HOW TO BUILD YOUR CHRISTIAN CHARACTER

HOW TO BUILD YOUR CHRISTIAN CHARACTER

Stanley C. Baldwin

This book is designed for your personal reading pleasure and profit. It is also designed for group study. A Leader's Guide with helps and hints for teachers and with visual aids (Victor Multiuse Transparency Masters) is available from your local bookstore or from the publisher.

VICTOR BOOKS a division of SP Publications, Inc.

WHEATON. ILLINOIS 60187

Offices also in
Whitby, Ontario, Canada
Amersham-on-the-Hill, Bucks, England

Fourth printing, 1985

Most Old Testament quotations are from the *New American Standard Bible* (NASB), © 1960, 1962, 1963, 1968, 1971, 1973 by the Lockman Foundation, La Habra, California; most New Testament quotations are from the *New International Version* (NIV), © 1978 by the New York Bible Society. Other quotations are from the *King James Version* (KJV) and *The Living Bible* (LB), © 1971 by Tyndale House Publishers.

Recommended Dewey Decimal Classification: 227.93
  Suggested Subject Heading: BIBLE, N.T. 2 PETER

Library of Congress Catalog Card Number: 81-52240
ISBN: 0-88207-271-4

VICTOR BOOKS
A division of SP Publications, Inc.
      Wheaton, Illinois 60187

Contents

to Marge
wife, companion, adviser, friend,
fellow-searcher after truth

Preface

It is always somewhat threatening to write about great truths, for doing so implies a claim that I know them. Some who observe me may feel that "Maybe he knows it, but he seldom shows it."

God will ultimately be the Judge. I can only say that this book was born out of a deep personal conviction of the importace of character-building and with an earnest desire to truly help God's people in that great undertaking.

I owe a debt of gratitude:

- to Jim Adair, Executive Editor of Victor Books, who encouraged me to write this book and gave early guidance on some of its content.
- to my wife Marge, who always took time to listen when I needed to sort out an issue and who helped me hammer out a balanced presentation of the truth.
- to the members of the writers critique group to which I belong. They supported me, prayed for me, and patiently critiqued this book, chapter by chapter. My thanks goes to each of them: Gloria Chisholm, Gail Denham, Birdie Etchison, Janice Hermansen, Sally Stuart, and Marjorie Zimmerman, with added thanks to Elaine Morgan for her special prayer interest and to Caryl Silverthorne for her contribution of anecdotes.
- to the listeners of "Truth For Our Times," the radio broadcast on which much of this material was first presented, and to the churches which have entrusted me with the privilege of ministering to their people, at the same time helping me to grow and learn.

Having received so much help from so many, I offer this work now with great anticipation and hope. May God find it useful to His glory and to the benefit of His people.

Part 1
The Importance of Character-Building

1
A Prophetic Look at Your Personal Future

Mention prophecy and Christians tend to think about Armageddon, the tribulation, antichrist, and Israel.

- Will the next war be fought over Middle East oil and turn out to be Armageddon?
- Will the tribulation come while Christians are still in this world to go through it?
- What is the identity of the antichrist and the significance of the number 666?
- What's going on behind the scenes in Israel, especially in regard to rebuilding the temple?

Some fine-tune their prophetic interest. They talk darkly about current political leaders, about plans to assign every person in the world a number, about mind-control and new currencies and gold.

I went with a friend into a bookstore in Salt Lake City. I like to talk with booksellers because they have daily contact with the people who buy books. As a Bible teacher and writer, I need all the grass-roots input I can get.

This bookseller impressed me. He had the professional air of one who knows his business, and I listened carefully to his comments about what books people are buying.

"Consistently near the top of the list," he said, "especially in uncertain times, are books on prophecy. Not just any prophetic book sells, but one that ties current events with Scripture—the newspaper with the Bible—that kind of book goes fast."

It's not difficult to understand why prophecy is big. Prophecy is captivating because it's about *us* and it's about our future. Few things interest us more.

The Most Significant Prophecy in the Bible

There is an often overlooked prophecy far more important to your personal life than anything mentioned so far.

It's true! If you are a Christian, there is a prophecy so focused on your life that when you fully grasp it, *everything you do will be affected*. This has to be the most exciting, the most significant, the most life-changing of all the stupendous prophecies of Scripture.

God looked down through time and saw *you*. Not just as one person among billions caught up in end-time events, but you, individually and personally. And *God foretold your future*. Astounding as that may be, it's true. And then the Lord went even further and revealed something of how your daily actions and choices would affect that future.

The great prophecy of which I speak is expressed in different ways and in many places in the Bible. One example is Romans 8:29:

> For those God foreknew He also predestined to be conformed to the likeness of His Son, that He might be the firstborn among many brothers.

You are to become like Jesus. That is part of the prophecy. You are also destined for a place in the future kingdom "among many brothers."

This prophecy could not possibly relate to you more personally than it does. It is very *you*. It is also *now*, for while the final fulfillment of it lies in the future, God's intention is to develop Christlike character in you here and now. In fact, that is God's overriding concern. Whatever happens in your life, good or bad, God seeks to use it to build your character (Rom. 8:28).

Note how this same theme comes through in Peter's second epistle, a letter given almost wholly to prophecy. We read (2 Peter 3:13), "In keeping with His promise, we are looking forward to . . . "

To what?

The economic collapse of the West?

A Middle-East oil war?

A Russian invasion of Israel?

Worldwide famine?

Nuclear holocaust?

No, none of these is the focus, though Peter has just described a destruction by fire that sounds much like a nuclear holocaust (3:10-12). Now he follows that immediately by saying, "In keeping with His promise, we are looking forward to *a new heaven and a new earth, the home of righteousness*" (v. 13). And he follows that, in turn, by saying, "Since you are looking forward to this, make every effort to be found spotless, blameless, and at peace with Him" (v. 14).

Do you see it?

The most significant prophecy is:

God is establishing a new order, a righteous brotherhood, for which each of us should be diligently preparing.

Now.

We must not get so taken up with the mechanics by which this present system is passing away that we lose sight of the grand destiny to which we are moving and therefore fail to prepare ourselves.

Lining Up with God's Purposes

The prophetic Scriptures tell us clearly what God has in mind for us ultimately. "Just as we have borne the likeness of the earthly man [Adam], so we shall bear the likeness of the man from heaven [Christ]" (1 Cor. 15:49).

As we have said, God is working continually, even now, to conform us to the likeness of His Son. If we want to cooperate with God, then, we must seek the same thing He seeks, our growth in Christlikeness.

Is that your goal? Or are you off on some tangent?

Most of us tend to muddle along mindlessly. Maybe we move in God's direction, and maybe we don't, but whichever happens, it's by accident. We get busy doing our own thing and don't bother to inquire what God's thing for us is.

When we do inquire about God's will, we fail to ask the most important question. We ask what we should *do* but not what we should *be*. We ask how we should change our *circumstances* but not how we should change our *characters*.

We Christians are told to become like Jesus. If God puts this uppermost, surely we should be seeking the same thing. I mean, really working at it.

But what if we don't?

What difference does it make anyhow? When we leave this earth, won't we become just like Jesus instantly? Won't we, therefore, become all we could possibly be? Why struggle and sacrifice to make slow progress toward a goal that God will accomplish for us all at once when we get to glory?

Good questions. We'll explore more fully what it means to be "like Christ" in chapter 4 of this book. To seek some other light on what will happen when we leave this life, let's look now into the prophecies about the coming judgment of each believer.

Many Christians have only a fuzzy idea of what to expect hereafter. To some degree this is unavoidable, for the Bible does not spell everything out for us. However, we can at least know what the Bible does say.

Christians Will Be Judged on Character

Important insight into what will happen to believers hereafter is found in 2 Corinthians 5:10:

> For we must all appear before the Judgment Seat of Christ, that
> each one may receive what is due him for the things done while
> in the body, whether good or bad.

This verse requires careful examination. The original Greek uses an entirely different word for *judgment* here than for the judgment of unbelievers, because this is a whole different scene.

For example, Peter writes that God will "hold the unrighteous for the day of judgment [*krisis*], while continuing their punishment" (2 Peter 2:9).

By contrast, Paul writes about the believer standing before "the judgment seat" [*bema*] to "receive what is due him" (2 Cor. 5:10). This passage does not mention punishment, for a justified person has no sins to his account for which to be punished (Rom. 4:4-8).

Some insight as to what will transpire at the *bema* may be gained by considering the expression, "we must all appear" there (2 Cor. 5:10). This is not the best translation, for it sounds as if we who are Christians will only show up, or put in an appearance. What it actually says is that we shall be manifested; what we truly are will become open and apparent.

Does this begin to give you a hint why it's important to develop Christian character? The exact degree to which you have or have not done so will be revealed at the *bema*. That could be embarrassing.

Next we are told that this will occur "that each one may receive what is due him for the things done while in the body." Why must our characters be revealed *in order that* (as the Greek has it) our deeds may be judged? Because actions cannot be properly appraised apart from the motives behind them. This is true of good deeds as well as bad. Thus, "though I bestow all my goods to feed the poor, and though I give my body to be burned, and have not love, it profiteth me nothing" (1 Cor. 13:3, KJV).

To what degree your good deeds were rightly motivated will be made known when you appear before the *bema*. To what degree your misdeeds were acts of malice and other bad motives will also be revealed then.

We will each receive his due "for the things done." What the Greek says literally is, "For the things *practiced*." Once again we are back to the issue of character, for a person may commit an act that is uncharacteristic of him, but his practice flows from his nature, from what he is.

At the *bema*, then, character will be the paramount issue. But there is more.

Taking Up Where We Left Off

Paul's wording (2 Cor. 5:10) seems to suggest not only that we will be judged on character but also that we will take up where we left off here in some respects.

How does the verse suggest that? By Paul's curious choice of language. Our text says each one will "receive what is due him for the things done while in the body," but the original omits "what is due him" and simply says each one is to "receive the things done in the body."

A parable may help here.

A young man was taken on by his father-in-law, a homebuilder, who taught him all he knew. One day the older man said to his son-in-law, "I'd like you to take charge of building a home for a very special client. Everything is to be first class. Spare no pains."

The builder then went away on other business so the young man knew he was in complete control. To celebrate his new status, he threw a party one night. Many subcontractors were among his guests, as were potential future customers. The subcontractors saw in the young man a source of business for themselves, so they were most friendly. Various ones invited him to breakfast.

The young man, in turn, wanted to win the potential customers, so he planned more ways to entertain them. It was all so exciting that the house he was building seemed relatively dull stuff.

He did keep at the job, after a fashion, but since he was distracted he became careless here and there. Inside the walls, where they could not be seen, he used inferior materials, diverting the money saved to "entertaining clients." He knew the house would look just as good, and he refused to think about the defects that would begin showing up after the house was occupied.

At last the house was finished, and his father-in-law

returned. "Let's inspect the place before I turn it over to the new owner," he said. The two of them walked through the house, which looked quite good. At the front door, as they were leaving, the father-in-law reached into his jacket pocket for an envelope which he handed the young man. "Congratulations, son," he said, "here is the title to your new home. You are the special client for whom I wanted a well-built house. May you enjoy many happy years here."

You see, God has assigned us a building project too, and we just may find at the *bema* that we will have to live with the result, that we will "receive . . . the things done while in the body, whether good or bad."

Instant Perfection—Will It Ever Happen?

How can it be that we will in any sense take up in the next life where we leave off here? Aren't we going to be perfect in heaven?

Well, there certainly won't be any sin there. We know that for sure (Rev. 21:27). So, yes, we will be perfect in that sense at least.

But there is another consideration. Perhaps we should be thinking not in terms of perfection but of capacity.

David Needham, in his book *Birthright,** compares believers to diamonds.

> Life here on earth is . . . the time during which God adds new facets to His original, flawless diamond—you. . . . The sanctifying miracle of the new birth guarantees the quality of the diamond. But you and I have a most responsible role to play in determining the . . . facets as we willingly submit to the Master Diamond Cutter.

What Needham suggests is that one may have perfection in heaven and still be far less than he might have been—few-faceted instead of many-faceted, as it were.

Neglecting to become all we can become in this life will have serious effects then. Either it will put us behind in a development that continues in the next life, or, far worse, it may diminish us forever.

---

*©1979 by Multnomah Press, Portland, Oregon.

Let's think about this subject from a little different viewpoint. Think of a person who *has* faithfully developed his capacities. Is he to be no better off in eternity for it? Wilbur M. Smith in his book *The Biblical Doctrine of Heaven,** seems to indicate otherwise, quoting the "famous French writer" Louis Figuier:

> The brilliant tribute of knowledge, intellect, and varied faculties which man has acquired at the cost of so many efforts cannot be taken from him. He will retain them when he passes to the farther side of the tomb.
>
> Mozart died at 35, after amazing and delighting his contemporaries by the productions of his precocious genius; and shall his genius and his personality vanish forever because death prematurely arrested his earthly career? We cannot think so. . . .
>
> Raphael at 37 dropped into the night of the tomb the brush which had created so many masterpieces, and must he therefore stop short in his sublime career? No! His soul continues, doubt it not, to scatter masterpieces among the happy beings who people the ethereal fields.
>
> Why does the old man, near his end, still cherish hopes which seem foolish and ridiculous to everyone else? Because he has a vague and secret presentiment that after the shadows of the evening of life shall come the bright lights of a new dawn, and a hope that the plans which he secretly ponders may someday be realized.
>
> It is not in vain that he has labored and suffered here below; his experience and his wisdom shall not be taken from him. Then let him dream, during his last days of life, of enterprises to be realized when he has crossed the terrible bridge that leads to eternity.

Figuier is saying one will not lose the capacities developed in this life, and he applies this to a typical "old man" as well as to such geniuses as Mozart and Raphael. I am saying that, by the same token, one will not instantly gain all the capacities left undeveloped in this life. Figuier implies as much when he says

---

*© 1968 by Moody Press, Chicago, Ill.

of the "old man," "It is not in vain that he has labored and suffered here below; his experience and his wisdom shall not be taken from him." If an equivalent wisdom were indiscriminately given to everyone, it would be in vain that he labored and suffered. He'd have enjoyed exactly the same result anyhow.

It comes down to a rather simple principle. If you've worked to become all you can be here, you'll keep the results there. If you haven't, don't expect it all to be given to you.

One thing we know for sure. Our works as believers will be tried "with fire," and if they do not stand the test we will definitely "suffer loss" (1 Cor. 3:11-15).

One Other Thing

Apart from any concerns about future judgment, there is another reason you and I should seek to become like our Lord Jesus Christ. It is the same reason a child seeks and longs to become an adult. That is its nature.

It is the nature of a believer to grow toward Christlikeness. If you are not interested in doing so, it means either that you do not understand who you are as a Christian, or you are not one.

But as the Scripture says, "Even though we speak like this, dear friends, we are confident of better things in your case—things that accompany salvation" (Heb. 6:9).

I believe you want to line up with God's purpose in your life and that down deep you care much about the kind of person you are becoming. I believe that if you understand the importance of building Christian character, if you know what to aim at and how to proceed, you will get on with the work.

And that is what this book is all about.

2
Just When You Find the Answers, How Come the Questions Change?

In chapter 1, I mentioned an insightful bookseller in Salt Lake City who said that prophetic books are often his bestsellers. The second high-interest category he mentioned is *how-to* books. People are looking for answers.

With this in mind, I went to the public library to see how many how-to books are on the market. Consulting a handy little two-volume 4,530-page publication called *Books in Print,* I found an incredible 3,500 plus how-to titles. And that does not include all the how-to books with other titles, such as *You Can* . . . or *The Art of.* . . .

Among the 3,500 how-to titles, I found some
29 *How to Succeed* . . .
65 *How to Win* . . .
87 *How to Live* . . .
140 *How to Get* . . .
172 *How to Be* . . .
Some of the more curious titles I noticed were:

How to Be a Pregnant Father. As soon as I saw that one I began compiling a mental list of all the men I knew who needed it. I concluded that I could give each one a free copy and suffer little damage to my meager bank account. I calculated my cost would be about the same as the amount the Communist Party spends each year on Christian missions.

How to Become King. I really wanted a copy of this book when I first saw the title, but then I got to thinking. If I became a king, it would make all the neighbors jealous. Besides, I really look dumb wearing a hat, and I doubt that a crown would look much better.

How to Be Sexy with Bugs in Your Teeth. No doubt a helpful manual for the happy smiling motorcyclist with an amorous streak. But I don't really ride my good old Suzuki that much (especially since my son wrecked it—and his left knee—the other day).

How to Be a Better Past Life Regression Receiver. Sounds like a barrel of fun, but I'll pass. This life—and the next—are quite enough for me, thank you.

The librarian was beginning to look at me a bit suspiciously. Not used to seeing people laugh out loud anywhere in the Reference section, I suppose, and especially while plowing through *Books in Print*.

I decided to leave but not before checking for one more title. I had some trouble finding it—there are more than 3,500 how-to titles—but I felt in my innermost being it had to be there. At last, my faith rewarded, I went peaceably, the eyes of the librarian following me to the door. I can now tell you definitely. Yes, Virginia, there is a book entitled, *How to Write How-To Articles*.

A Trouble-Free Life?

With more than 3,500 how-to books in print, it seems the person who knows *how to* read ought to be able to breeze through almost anything. Alas, it is not so.

For one thing, with most of us there is considerable gap between knowing and doing. We are like the farmer who was resisting the sales pitch of a magazine peddler. "Why, sir," said the peddler, "with this magazine you'll be able to farm at least 50% more efficiently than you have in the past. Now, isn't it worth just pennies a day for that kind of results?"

Unimpressed, the old farmer shook his head slowly. "Won't help," he said. "I already know how to farm 100% better than I'm doin' it."

Knowing how doesn't assure that we will do as well as we know, whether it's in farming or in living. That's where character comes in. Yet the books on character-building can be counted on the fingers of both hands. Isn't that a huge imbalance?

There is another reason why so many how-to books will not lead to a trouble-free life. Stated bluntly, solving one problem or 3,500 of them never exhausts the supply. Life deals out new difficulties as fast as we can resolve the old ones, and sometimes a lot faster. However great our resources, then, there simply is no such thing as a placid, no-problems life. About the time we think we've found our answers, the questions change. We must start at "Go" all over again (and we don't always collect $200 either).

You see, God's program is not designed to minimize our difficulties but to maximize our character development. He doesn't intend to eliminate the mountains from our path but to give us strength to climb them. He's not trying to make the way smooth so much as to make the wayfarer sturdy. His first question is not, "Will this contribute to an easier life for My child?" but, "Will this make his character more Christlike?"

The Flying Sparks Principle

In the Book of Job, we read that "man is born for trouble as sparks fly upward" (Job 5:7). Believe me, sparks do fly upward. I discovered that when I experienced a bonfire recently, something I hadn't done in years. In sprucing up a small wooded acreage we own, I had accumulated a huge supply of fir boughs, apple branches, and berry vines. When a day came that the Department of Environmental Quality gave the OK, I started burning them. It was dusk by the time I threw the last big pile of clippings on the fire. The shower of sparks flying high into the night air was a sight to behold. Remembering Job, I thought, *Wow, if trouble is as natural to our lives as flying sparks are to that fire, it's no wonder we have our hands full.*

A contemporary saying paralleling the one from Job is Murphy's Law: "If something can go wrong, it will." Some cynic has added, "And Murphy was an optimist."

That may sound a bit overstated and no doubt it is. But it also strikes close to home. Tasks I undertake almost always involve unforeseen difficulties.

Just yesterday, for example, I became discouraged and exasperated in attempting a minor home improvement project. We have a small feature wall in our entry, and I undertook to cover it with foot-square mirror tiles. It's a simple process. You affix a one-inch-square of rubber, sticky on both sides, to each corner of a mirror tile and press it against the wall. Nothing to it. Except that the wall needs to be perfectly flat. Otherwise, each of the mirror tiles assumes a slightly different plane and the resulting image is distorted.

After so many hours of trying to compensate for irregularities on the wall surface by inserting slivers of wood here and there, putting the tile up again and again only to find that solving the problem with one tile aggravated it with the next, I felt like making mirror fragments of the whole mess.

Responses to Trouble

There are a number of ways I could have reacted to this mild encounter with the flying sparks principle, or Murphy's Law.

1. I could have quit. That would have meant giving up on the mirror tiles, and just painting the wall since paint does not require a perfectly flat surface.

To me this is usually not an acceptable alternative. I guess I was taught to finish whatever I started. Besides, I have a stubborn streak, a kind of pride which demands that no simple undertaking will get the best of me. But there is more to it than that. If I quit simply because it's too hard, what will keep me from quitting all along the line? It's the nature of life to encounter trouble everywhere, remember? This brings us to my next possible reaction.

2. I could have quit in a more profound sense. I could give up all do-it-yourself projects around the house. Carrying my "I quit" even further, I could give up trying to do anything except safe, easy, no-challenge tasks with which I am thoroughly familiar.

The profound "I quit" is what many people have said at some point in life. Thus they attempt to avoid the flying sparks principle by walking away from the fire. This is nothing less than tragic for it runs directly counter to God's purpose for us.

As we have said, a trouble-free life is not what God is trying to provide. He wants us to become strong in character and He knows that struggling with difficulties, persisting in the face of discouragement, and attaining our goals through faith and perseverance, builds character. We will speak more of this in chapters 5, 8, and 9, which discuss adding endurance to our faith.

For now, let us simply determine that our desire for peace and tranquility and ease and painless living must not take precedence over our desire for growth. As the *Living Bible* puts it:

> Dear brothers, is your life full of difficulties and temptations? Then be happy, for when the way is rough, your patience has a chance to grow. So let it grow, and don't try to squirm out of your problems. For when your patience is finally in full bloom, then you will be ready for anything, strong in character, full and complete (James 1:2-4).

This passage rules out the profound "I quit" reaction to difficulty. What other alternatives did I have in the case of the mirror tiles?

3. I could have withdrawn temporarily. Sometimes I get emotionally overwhelmed by my problems. To doggedly keep at a project risks burnout or explosion. If those misplaced mirror tiles stared crookedly at me one more time, there might have been violence, or tears.

OK, I may withdraw. I'm yielding nothing, you understand. I'll be back. And I will prevail. But right now I'm going to do something else. Maybe there will be problems with that other activity too—there are days like that—but at least it will be a different set of problems.

It's OK too if I simply need to relax, to do nothing but recharge my batteries for a while.

The Bigger Hammer Principle
I had yet another alternative in my mirror-tile tussle:

4. I could have employed the "bigger hammer" principle. I once worked as a maintenance mechanic in a large industrial plant. If we had trouble—in dismantling a piece of machinery, for example—we would say, "We've got to get a bigger hammer." This expression was based on the facetious premise that if something won't come loose or doesn't work, you just hit it. If it still doesn't yield, you hit it harder. Get a bigger hammer.

More than one person has followed this advice literally, with vending machines, television sets, auto batteries, and various home appliances being literally beaten to scrap as a result.

Despite this obvious abuse, the bigger hammer principle is partially sound. If you are having difficulty, bring greater resources to bear on the undertaking. Get help. The additional resource may consist of:

● Better tools. It's tough to overhaul a car with a screwdriver and a pair of pliers. Or to cook a gourmet meal with one frying pan and a hot plate.

● More manpower. Some jobs require three hands instead of two. Considering the way the Creator designed us, He must have intended for us to seek and to give help in such situations.

● More know-how. Some of those 3,500 how-to books do have value. And so do friends and relatives. Almost everyone you know is a walking how-to book in some field.

We have said, then, that when trouble comes, as it inevitably does, we can:

● Quit on that particular project.
● Quit on a life of achievement generally.
● Withdraw temporarily to return stronger than ever.
● Acquire greater resources and prevail.

We are in danger of taking the second and most harmful alternative when, thinking only about the pain associated with the undertaking, we tell ourselves it is not worth it.

The Two-Birds-with-One-Stone Principle

It is important to keep in mind, when difficulties arise, that no matter what we are attempting to accomplish, another and more important project is going forward at the same time. Yesterday I was not only putting mirror tile on my wall. I was also experiencing the testing and building of my character. At this moment I am not only writing a book about building character, I am also doing it, because, believe me, this is not an easy or trouble-free task. (Shall I tell you about my recalcitrant typewriter?)

Remembering that you are killing two birds with one stone whenever you seek to accomplish anything really helps. It doesn't totally eliminate the frustration, but it does keep it from turning into bitterness and resentment.

Earlier I cited James 1:2: "Dear brothers, is your life full of difficulties and temptations? Then be happy." This does not mean that you should cope so well that nothing bothers you. If it didn't bother you, it would not be a temptation.

Are you always serene? Always smiling? Always saying "Praise the Lord," in your heart? If you are continually "up" like that, you are going Jesus one better. He wept on two occasions that we know of and other times groaned in great heaviness.

"Be happy" when trials come? I can tell you I wasn't all smiles at the peak of my mirror-tile exasperation. And that trouble was relatively trivial—though in another sense anguish is anguish, whatever its cause. Anyhow, when I keep in mind that God is developing my character through trials (whether momentous or seemingly inconsequential), I do experience a joy that underlies all the surface emotions and gives me strength to go on interacting with my world. This, I believe, is what James was writing about.

You see, some "Praise the Lord anyhow" people seem always "up," but when you look closely at their lives you may see withdrawal. They are evading difficulty, not overcoming it. How? By sidestepping whatever may be difficult or demanding. This is symptomatic of a person who does not grasp either the urgency or the dynamic of character-building.

I do not suggest that anyone court suffering. Nor should we undertake tasks at which we are sure to fail just because it might be good for us to try them. The two-birds-with-one-stone principle implies accomplishment of *both* goals. But the possibility of failure must not deter us from an undertaking, for even our failures can be valuable to us in terms of character growth, and that is what is most important.

Sweet Music in Our Souls

Just what does it mean to build Christian character? What are the elements of this character and how do they fit together? The Apostle Peter writes:

> Make every effort to add to your faith goodness; and to goodness, knowledge; and to knowledge, self-control; and to self-control, perseverance; and to perseverance, godliness; and to godliness, brotherly kindness; and to brotherly kindness, love (2 Peter 1:5-7).

This admonition to add to faith, goodness, and so on, can be compared to a musical chord. The character traits are more like different notes in a full harmonic chord than like rungs on a ladder. "*In* your faith, add goodness" comes closer to Peter's thought than "*to* your faith, add goodness."

The point is that we are to develop all these traits at the same time, because each one augments all the others. The object is to "possess these qualities in increasing measure," as verse 8 reads. We don't wait until our goodness is complete and then start working on knowledge, and so on. No, we constantly seek to add more and more of each trait until our whole life crescendos into a symphony to God. It is thus we avoid the trap of which G. G. Findlay writes:

> We are apt to become specialists in virtue as in other departments of life. Men will endeavor even to compensate by extreme efforts in one direction for deficiencies in some other direction, which they scarcely desire to make good. So they grow out of shape, into oddities and moral malformations. . . . We have sweetness without strength, and strength without gentleness, and truth spoken without love, and words of passionate zeal without accuracy and heedfulness. . . . Let us never imagine that our defects in one kind will be atoned for by

excellences in another. Our friends may say this, in charity for us; it is a fatal thing when a man begins to say so to himself.*

By contrast, as we add all the qualities Peter cites, we become God's song, composed by the Lord Himself and rich with the harmony of a well-blended character. What an exciting destiny! What a worthwhile goal!

---

*From *What Makes You So Special?* by Stanley C. Baldwin; © 1977, Baker Book House, Grand Rapids, Michigan.

Part 2
Seven Traits of Christian Character

from 2 Peter 1:5-7

3
Being Good
without Being
Goody-Goody

The first character trait Peter lists and the first we want to consider is virtue, or goodness. Peter writes, "Make every effort to add to your faith goodness" (2 Peter 1:5).

Two brothers, Fred and Ed, were neighboring farmers, as the story goes. Ed was a decent fellow, even devout in a private way, but he seldom went to church, and had his full share of bad habits. Fred, on the other hand, was very religious and scrupulous. He was present every time the doors opened at his church, and he was so "righteous" that most people felt uncomfortable being around him.

It seemed Fred was always having bad fortune. His equipment broke down oftener, his crops failed more and suffered worse insect infestations than his "loose-living" brother's. When these things happened, Fred consoled himself by saying, "Many are the afflictions of the righteous," and then he redoubled his efforts to be good.

One day things came to a head. On top of everything else that was going wrong, Fred was caught on his tractor in a sudden, violent thunderstorm. He was drenched, and half frightened to death. Alighting from the tractor, he began a dash for cover but slipped and went sprawling on his face in the mud. Slowly he rose to his hands and knees. Then, looking up to heaven, he cried out, "Why, Lord? Why does everything happen to me?"

A voice came back, "Fred, there's just something about you that ticks Me off."

Well, how does the story strike you? Frankly, it bothers me. It seems irreverent to put such words in the mouth of God. On the other hand, I think the story does make a valid point. Some people are so goody-goody they even turn off God. There's a $64 word for it—*sanctimonious,* which means affecting piousness or being hypocritically devout.

But watch out for that word *hypocritical.* If it only means pretending to be what you know you are not, it doesn't fit Fred. He was sincere. But since *hypocritical* means "playing a part, as on the stage," that's different. That does fit Fred. Though he was sincere, he was playing the part of a perfect person, which he was not.

We might say, then, that there is such a thing as "sincere hypocrisy." One can be a phony in some ways and not even know it.

A listener who heard me present much of the content of this chapter on the radio program "Truth For Our Times" responded as follows:

> What an attitude you have! Calling non-sinners goody-goody! It seems that more credit is given to a reformed sinner than to the person who has resisted temptations.
>
> I'm sure a Christian knows that God forgives the sinner if he is truly repentant. You make it sound like one could very well indulge in wrongdoing just so he could repent and be able to put himself in the other person's place so he won't appear to be self-righteous.
>
> Don't knock morality! One should feel some pride in goodness. Better to err on that side than to slip into Satan's trap. Soon we become tolerant and close our eyes to all sorts of "little" sins. It has happened with regard to premarital births, pornographic TV, kids' smoking areas in our schools, etc.

I responded by condemning the notion that one should sin in order to seem less self-righteous. I apologized if I had left that impression.

But as for my calling "non-sinners" goody-goody, I said,

ch a phenomenon suggests that somewhere along the line
e message has not been heard: "Make every effort to add to
ur faith goodness."

If you as a Christian have not concerned yourself with being
od, this is where you must begin. Goodness is foundational
Christian character.

oodness with a Backbone

hen Peter writes, "Add to your faith goodness," he uses a
rd seldom found in Scripture. The common word for good is
athos, which appears some 102 times in the New Testament.
t Peter tell us to add *arete*, which according to *Young's
ncordance* literally means strength or force. *Arete* is used
ly five times in Scripture, four of these in the Epistles of
ter. Two of these four times, Peter uses the word to describe
e Lord Himself ("praises," 1 Peter 2:9; "goodness," 2 Peter
3).

The other two times Peter uses the word *arete*, it is to
scribe this trait we are to add to our faith—namely, the
rong kind of goodness that is attributed to God Himself.

Peter understood, perhaps better than any of the other
ostles, that a simple disposition toward goodness is not
ough. There must also be the strength to follow through on
at disposition. A person of character is one who has both
nvictions and the courage of those convictions.

Peter understood this so well because he once lacked such
odness so tragically. It was no shortage of good disposition
at made Peter fail. His words were not mere bluster when he
ld Jesus he would die with Him rather than deny Him. He
ncerely and intensely loved his Lord. In the garden, when an
med mob led by Judas came to arrest Jesus, it was Peter who
ew his sword and fought alone in Jesus' defense, hopeless as
e odds were against him.

But whatever goodness Peter had, it was not enough.
ossibly his act of heroism drained the little strength that was
him. Then, the reservoir empty, he lacked any more
pacity to fight, or even to stand. As Jesus was led away

there are no such people. Non-sinners don't exist—only
people so proud or so blind that they cannot see their sin.

With regard to it being "better to err" on the side of the
goody-goody, I asked why we should err on either side.
Indeed, that is the whole point I'm trying to make—that we can
and should be good without being goody-goody.

As for becoming tolerant of "little" sins, I felt obliged to point
out that all of the sins cited by my critic seemed clearly to be
the *sins of others*. I was confident that neither the offended
listener nor I was into "premarital births, pornographic TV, or
kids' smoking areas."

I suggested that true goodness does not so much require
intolerance of other people's sins as it does intolerance of our
own. A list that includes resentment, indifference to others'
suffering, hostility, indulgence in overeating, and a critical and
unloving spirit might be more appropriate, if indeed we are
talking about the subject of our *own* personal goodness.

So then, being goody-goody really is a danger. To say so is
not a matter of trying to excuse loose living by pointing a finger
at those who are more rigid.

Jesus' own example makes this clear, for He, the sinless Son
of God, was often at odds with the goody-goody phonies of His
day. They criticized Him for everything from eating with
unwashed hands to working on the Sabbath. He in turn
castigated them for their hypocrisy. Most of Matthew 23 is a
record of the woes He pronounced on such people. Early in
that denunciation, we find this significant charge: "They tie up
heavy loads and put them on men's shoulders, but they
themselves are not willing to lift a finger to move them" (Matt.
23:4).

Jesus Himself thus provides a test for the validity of our
goodness. Is it the kind that makes us compassionate? Or does
it tend more toward arrogance? Do we lighten the loads of
those around us? Or do we increase their burdens?

June was brought up in a strict home and taught, among
other things, that the wearing of jewelry was unspiritual. For
her 16th birthday, the young people in her church gave June a

party. June opened her gifts, appropriately thanking each giver, until out of one small package she pulled a necklace. It was a gift from Mary, a sensitive newcomer to the group, who had only gone to church a few times.

"Oh, I can't accept this," June said, plopping it back in Mary's hands. "I don't believe in wearing jewelry."

June came out of that little experience feeling quite virtuous. She had taken her stand for righteousness. Mary came out carrying a load of false guilt and rejection, which June laid on her and never moved a finger to lift.

I'm not suggesting that June should have compromised her convictions. She didn't have to wear the jewelry in order to accept it in the spirit in which it was given. And if she felt compelled to make her stand known, she could have done that too. She could have accepted the gift with thanks, and explained to individuals privately, later on, what her convictions were. Or she might have declined the gift in a manner so gracious it would not have reflected on the giver.

It is said of Richelieu that he was so gracious that a man asked him a favor he had no expectation of receiving, just to hear Richelieu say no. We wouldn't expect the same perfected grace in a teenager, but we could hope for some of the same spirit.

Jesus in His perfect goodness was always mindful of the needs of people. And He had severe words for those whose "goodness" was divorced from compassion. We'll learn more about what God calls Christian character in this regard when we study brotherly kindness, for remember that every quality Peter exhorts us to add is moderated by every other quality, a harmonious blend being God's plan for us.

Needed: Good Christians Who Are Also Good People

Fred and Ed and June notwithstanding, God does expect His own to be good people, doesn't He? The Bible does say, "Everyone who confesses the name of the Lord must turn away

from wickedness" (2 Tim. 2:19). The same ve that this concept is foundational to the king

Foundational or not, however, goodness automatically with Christian faith. If it did, admonish us to add it, making every effort

As we observe people, we discover they va this regard. Some, when they are conve immediately demonstrate a profound moral don't show much initial change in lifestyle, e have just as much or far more need to do so, v sin in their lives.

Zaccheus was a man who showed renewal. come down from his perch in the tree to receiv when he declared, "Here and now I give half o to the poor, and if I have cheated anybody ou will pay back four times the amount" (Luke

However, an invalid at the pool of Beth dramatic healing, was warned by Jesus, "Se again. Stop sinning or something worse may (John 5:14). Assuming that Jesus would not needlessly, it seems this man had to be adm goodness to his faith.

Perhaps the clearest case of Christians goodness to faith is found in the citizens of the The preconversion lifestyle of these Cretians desired. They were described by one of their "always liars, evil brutes, lazy gluttons" (Titus Titus, whose task it was to minister to converts "This testimony is true. Therefore, rebuke th that they will be sound in the faith" (1:13).

The people of Crete needed more than ad add goodness to faith: they needed sharp rebu they were likely to continue in their old way

Some observers of our contemporary scene ed that in the United States, where millions citizens profess to be evangelical Christians, so becoming more Christian and less moral at t

prisoner, Peter sneaked along behind at a safe distance. And when various ones threatened to expose him as one of Jesus' disciples, he three times denied it, even with oaths and curses.

Yes, Peter knew that a person of character must have goodness with strength. He must have steel in his spine. (Remember, that's in his spine, not in his heart; Satan loves to reverse that.)

The Process

Where does one get this quality of strong goodness that Peter admonishes us to add to our faith? Oh, how easy it would be to write that you must get your goodness from God. This would sound properly spiritual, and few could fault me for saying something so unimpeachably true. However, it would also be a cop-out on my part and not too helpful to you as a reader. Of course God is the source of goodness, just as He is the source of health and energy and talent and skill and wisdom and our next breath and every other good thing. This is an important truth to keep in mind. But it is not a sufficient answer to offer anyone who wants to know how to get these things.

Peter does not resort to any such pious-sounding evasions. He of all people knew what it meant to fail when he depended on his own efforts. Nevertheless he writes, "*Make every effort* to add to your faith goodness" (2 Peter 1:5).

There are specific things we can do to develop goodness. Here are four:

1. *Make a definite choice*. Purpose that you will pursue goodness like Job, whom Scripture describes as "fearing God and turning away from evil" (Job 1:8).

Do not be halfhearted about this decision. Do not secretly reserve certain areas for sins you are unwilling to renounce. To do that is to sabotage the very goodness you seek.

Choosing goodness is not enough to produce goodness, as we have already noticed in the case of Peter's denial of the Lord Jesus. Yet it is the first prerequisite, and you will never make much progress without such a choice.

2. *Develop discernment of good and evil*. It should be clear

that one cannot consistently follow the good and avoid the evil if he can't tell which is which.

You may think this is no probem, that you intuitively know good from evil. Or that common sense readily distinguishes the two. Or that if there were any doubt, you could quickly resolve it by consulting the Scriptures.

None of these easy assumptions is true. We'll delve into the nature of this problem and some solutions to it in chapter 5, when we consider the need to add knowledge (in this case, of good and evil) to faith and goodness.

3. *Select good models*. Since Christian character is Christ-likeness, looking to Jesus as your model is the most helpful thing you can do. He exemplifies perfect goodness, devoid both of the sanctimonious spirit we warned about at the beginning of this chapter and of any complicity with evil. Be like Jesus and you will be good—guaranteed. Again, this concept will be elucidated further in the next chapter.

In addition to modeling your life after Jesus, you could get help from looking at other men and women of God. This has its dangers if you idolize such people, for in their humanity they are bound to fail sometimes. But if you will keep in mind their sinfulness, every good trait they reveal can be a source of inspiration and encouragement to you. For when you see genuine goodness in someone, you glimpse possibilities latent in yourself as well, for that person is only flesh and blood too. Your cry of faith ought to become, "If he can do it, by the grace of God so can I."

4. *Get strength from the Holy Spirit*. We've mentioned the need for "goodness with backbone" and observed how Peter once lacked the strength to follow through on his good intentions. Yet this same Peter, after he was filled with the Holy Spirit, exhibited great courage.

We too need and can have the Spirit's enabling power. It is not necessary to get tied in knots, as some have, trying to "make sure we are not acting in our own strength." Actually we should use all the "own strength" we have, as implied by the phrase, "Make every effort" (2 Peter 1:5). What is important is that we not stop there, as if our own strength were enough. Through prayer and a lively faith that claims God's promises, we must avail ourselves of that divine power that far supersedes our own.

As we commit ourselves to being good, learn more and more what true goodness is, model our lives after Jesus and other people of virtue, and draw on the power of Him who indwells us by His Spirit, we will succeed in adding goodness to our lives. We will be the better as a result.

4
Knowledge that Builds Up, Not Puffs Up

It is in some ways remarkable that Peter should write, "Add to your faith goodness; and to goodness, *knowledge*" (2 Peter 1:5). This man was no intellectual giant himself. Peter was a fisherman by trade, so he probably had little formal education.

This impression is confirmed to a degree by the comment in Acts 4:13 that Peter and John were "unschooled, ordinary men." This was in contrast to the elite Jewish leaders before whom they appeared at the time and should not be construed to imply that they were illiterates. After all, both of them later wrote important segments of the New Testament, and I'm sure they were neither ignorant nor unlearned in the popular sense.

Nevertheless, they were comparatively untutored and worked with their hands as fishermen, a condition sometimes associated with an anti-intellectual attitude.

It is worth noting in this connection that biblical warnings against "worldly wisdom" come mostly from the pen of the early church's most powerful and highly trained intellect, Paul, while this admonition to add knowledge comes from fisherman Peter.

That's good. It demonstrates how grace frees and balances people. When Paul writes about the limitations and pitfalls associated with learning, we know it's not just sour grapes. It's

42

not a case of ignorance talking about the liabilities of knowledge. When Peter writes about the importance of knowledge, he's not doing so from a position of superiority out of his own pride of formal learning, for he had little.

In any case, it is clear from Scripture that there is a knowledge that is no help to character. Paul writes that knowledge "puffs up" (1 Cor. 8:1). Which of us has not experienced the truth of that observation? One can even see it in children. Observe the self-important way in which a nine-year-old helps a seven-year-old with a word he can't decipher.

One can also see the puff-up potential of knowledge in the Christians at Corinth, who felt pretty smug about their grasp of the truth. They knew that idolatry is nonsense and that there is no God but one. As a result they tended to forget that others not so insightful could be hurt by their seeming disregard for separation from idolatry.

The arrogance, smugness, air of superiority, even disdain for "ignorant dolts" that may accompany knowledge makes it seem unlikely as a trait recommended to *improve* character.

This is seen rather clearly in the leaders of Jesus' day. Their knowledge made them incapable of learning anything from those they deemed inferior to themselves. Thus when the man born blind tried to reason with them about the implications of his healing, they replied, "You were steeped in sin at birth; how dare you lecture us!" (John 9:34)

Earlier, when many of the common people followed Jesus, the leaders showed their pride of learning by saying, "Has any of the rulers or of the Pharisees believed in Him? No! But this mob that knows nothing of the Law—there is a curse on them" (John 7:48-49).

From our vantage point, it appears the curse was on the learned, not on the ignorant. Yet Peter tells us to add knowledge to our faith and goodness.

How do we reconcile all of this? I believe that we can never really know too much. You see, while the learned and ignorant appear to be at opposite poles, they are often guilty of the same error. *Both fail to add knowledge*. The ignorant fail because they will not study or search or think, and may even take a perverse pride in being ignorant, as if they were better for it. The educated fail because they arrogantly assume they already know it all, or that they cannot learn from their "inferiors."

Peter speaks to both types and to all of us when he exhorts us to diligently add knowledge to our faith. Knowledge in three areas is especially critical to the building of Christian character. We will consider one of these areas in the remainder of this chapter.

We Must Know the Lord

This sounds deceptively simple, so I plead with you not to skim lightly over this concept assuming, "Yes, yes, I already know the Lord: I'm saved."

There is much more to it than that. Peter wrote, "*Grow* in the grace and knowledge of our Lord and Saviour Jesus Christ" (2 Peter 3:18). So even if you truly do know the Lord as your personal Saviour, you need to know Him better and better as you go on in life.

It is not just that this increasing knowledge would be nice, or that it would mark you as a spiritual Christian. More than that, there is a direct connection between how well you know the Lord and how successful you are in building Christian character.

Let me explain. Building Christian character involves becoming like the Lord Jesus Christ. *That's what Christian character is: Christlikeness*. One real hindrance to the advancement of that process is ignorance. We can hardly become like Christ if we don't know Him well enough to perceive what He is like.

This handicap will be with us to some degree as long as we live. That's why we read that when we see Him, "we shall be like Him, for we shall see Him as He is" (1 John 3:2). The idea is not necessarily that we shall then be instantaneously transformed into His perfect likeness. Rather, the thought seems to be that we can model ourselves to be closely like Him only when we see Him as He is.

As we observed in chapter 1, there is no assurance in Scripture that we will ever be granted instant and complete perfection in the sense of being all we could be. When we meet Jesus we will be perfectly sinless, but that doesn't mean we will be incapable of any further growth or development.

Someone may object, "But it says 'we shall be like Him,' not 'we shall be *more* like Him because we perceive Him more clearly.'"

In response to such an objection, I would point out that when the Bible says we will be "like Christ," that expression must *always* be understood relatively. It always means *more* like Him, because the day will never come when we will be exactly and altogether like Him.

Think for a moment. There are millions of Christians who will be "like Christ" in the age to come. Do you imagine any of us who will be mistaken for Him? Will there be nothing whatever to distinguish the multitudes from the Lord, or from one another? Are there to be millions of identical beings, all clones of Jesus?

No, no, no. He is forever the only begotten Son of God, unique and exalted above all others. We also are, and will always be, unique persons, each different from Him and from one another.

Right now we Christians are supposed to be changing, becoming more like Christ. But this process isn't magical. We are told exactly how it works. "But we all, with unveiled face beholding as in a mirror the glory of the Lord, are being transformed into the same image from glory to glory" (2 Cor. 3:18, NASB). We can see Christ in the mirror of His Word. We can come to know Him better as we read the Scriptures. But we can never know Him exactly as He is that way. "For now we see in a mirror dimly, but then face to face; now I know in part, but then I shall know fully just as I also have been fully known" (1 Cor. 13:12, NASB).

In chapter 1 we explained that at the judgment seat of Christ we will not simply "appear" but shall be manifested as we are. The same thing is true of our Lord Jesus Christ. The expression, "When He *appears*, we shall be like Him," ought to be translated, "When He is *manifested*, we shall be like Him" (1 John 3:2). What He really is will be known to us then, and that will make it possible for us to truly model ourselves after Him.

Peter writes that we should add knowledge to our faith not just because it would be nice, but because knowing Christ better is essential to becoming more like Him.

5
The Kinds of Knowledge You Need Most

In the previous chapter we spoke of the critical importance of adding to our faith an increasing knowledge of the Lord. Two other kinds of knowledge are especially important to character-building.

We Must Know Ourselves

To even use the expression "we must know ourselves" is suspect in the minds of some Christians. To them it smacks of psychology, humanism, narcissism. But what do the Scriptures say?

"Watch your life and doctrine closely. Persevere in them, because if you do, you will save both yourself and your hearers" (1 Tim. 4:16). We should be aware of what's going on inside of us. This is crucial both to our own spiritual welfare and to our service for Christ.

"For by the grace given me I say to every one of you: Do not think of yourself more highly than you ought, but rather think of yourself with sober judgment" (Rom. 12:3). We are to understand our true nature and characteristics.

"The heart is more deceitful than all else and is desperately sick; who can understand it? I the Lord search the heart, I test the mind, even to give to each man according to his ways,

47

according to the result of his deeds" (Jer. 17:9-10). We do not know ourselves automatically. We need help from without. This help must come from God, for He alone knows us completely and accurately. He searches our hearts, knows our minds, and judges our thoughts and attitudes (Heb. 4:12).

Peter himself was a graphic example of the lack of self-knowledge. Peter had, without a doubt, the initial spiritual enlightenment essential to salvation. That is, he knew who Jesus is. Others speculated that Jesus might be John the Baptist, Elijah, Jeremiah, or another Old Testament prophet returned. But Peter knew better. He said to Jesus, "You are the Christ, the Son of the living God" (Matt. 16:16). Jesus replied, significantly, that Peter was blessed because he had received this revelation from God. It wasn't simply a doctrine he had learned from man.

OK, so far so good. Peter at this point had faith—the prerequisite for being a Christian. But he needed to add to his faith goodness and knowledge—on the latter point particularly, some knowledge about Peter. For while Peter knew who Jesus is, he did not really know himself. This ignorance of who he was caused Peter severe difficulties, as foreshadowed in the immediate context of his great confession of faith. One has only to contrast Jesus' two statements to Peter:

Blessed are you, Simon, son of Jonah, for this was not revealed to you by man, but by My Father in heaven (Matt. 16:17).

Out of My sight, Satan! You are a stumbling block to Me; you do not have in mind the things of God, but the things of men (16:23).

Talk about mountain peak to valley's depth! And note that the very thing for which Peter was praised initially—spiritual insight—was what he was next denounced for lacking.

Peter had not lost his spiritual insight as to who Jesus is, but he clearly showed he didn't understand his own character when he took Jesus aside and rebuked Him (v. 22). Despite Jesus' correction at that time, Peter continued in his self-delusion. Later, when Jesus said that all the disciples would forsake Him, Peter flatly contradicted the Lord.

"Even if all fall away on account of You, I never will" (Matt. 26:33).

Yet before 24 hours had passed, Peter had denied the Lord 3 times. This in turn brought such a crisis into his life that he wept bitterly over his failure, and probably came close to losing his faith altogether. I say this because Jesus prayed especially for Peter, that his faith would not fail (Luke 22:32).

After the Resurrection, Jesus restored Peter and commissioned him to "feed My sheep" (John 21:15-17). In the process, however, Jesus asked searching questions designed to cause Peter to examine himself—to add self-knowledge to his faith and goodness.

In the English, one nuance of this exchange between Jesus and Peter is lost. The English language does not have words that exactly correspond to the original Greek. The *New American Standard Bible*, for one, brings out these distinctions in the margin.

To summarize, Jesus asked Peter three times, "Do you love Me?" Each time Peter affirmed that he did. However, in the Greek, two different words for love are used. The first two times, Jesus used the word meaning the highest and noblest form of love—*agapeo*. Peter answered each time using a weaker verb—*phileo*. This may seem out of character for Peter, a man not usually given to restraint or modest claims. But remember, this was a chastised Peter, to whom shameful failure was painfully fresh.

The third time Jesus asked the question, however, He switched to Peter's own term, *phileo*. The implication was that Peter needed to examine whether even his modest claim was valid. We must realize that the questions were asked to give Peter self-knowledge, not to inform Jesus of anything. He knew well enough what was in Peter.

Jesus asks us some penetrating questions as well, and for the same reason. As we read the Word of God, this remarkable mirror in which we see our Lord Jesus Christ, we may also see ourselves (see James 1:23-25). In prayer conversation with the Lord, we may hear Him asking us questions about our motives, our actions, our values, our priorities, our thoughts. He already knows us completely, but He wants us to know ourselves.

He further tells us that whenever we eat the Lord's Supper, we should examine ourselves (1 Cor. 11:28). Too much introspection certainly is not to be recommended. However, too little may leave us ignorant in a vital area where we ought to be adding knowledge to our faith.

Another way we can increase self-knowledge is to read the works of current popular psychologists. Of course we must not invest their writings with divine authority. We must weigh everything we read against the Word of God as interpreted to us by the Spirit of God. But it is a mistake to think we can learn nothing from secular sources. Paul did not assume there was no truth in such people. On the contrary, he not only read their works but sometimes cited pagan poets and philosophers with approval (see Acts 17:28 and Titus 1:12-13).

Still another way to increase self-knowledge is through confidential talks with a close Christian friend. A person who loves you enough to listen, being neither judgmental nor excusing, is a true blessing from God. You should seek both to have such a friend and to be one. It's what the Bible describes as true fellowship—walking in the light and bearing one another's burdens. (A helpful book relating to this and other "know yourself" concepts is *The Kink and I, a Psychiatrist's Guide to Untwisted Living*, by James D. Mallory, Jr. and Stanley C. Baldwin, Victor Books, Wheaton, Ill.)

Coming to know ourselves involves a certain degree of pain. We learn some things we really did not care to know. But these things are the very traits that mar our likeness to Jesus and distort our characters. We can't change in these areas if we don't even see what's wrong.

We Must Know Right and Wrong
A third kind of knowledge that builds character is the knowledge of right and wrong, of good and evil. Like knowing Jesus and knowing ourselves, this is easily but falsely assumed to be no problem.

Of course I know right from wrong, you think. *Everybody does unless he's perverted.*

Oh? Then how come the Bible speaks of "the mature, who by constant use have trained themselves to distinguish good from evil"? (Heb. 5:14) This verse certainly indicates that knowing good and evil requires both maturity and practice.

The difficulty of discerning good from evil helps explain why Christians line up on both sides of so many issues. Indeed, Christians of equal dedication may disagree on contemporary issues more often than not. Nor are these obscure, hair-splitting issues. They are as basic as, for example, Should our nation go to war? While most evangelicals would support a "just war" effort, great numbers would not, including some whole denominations.

Christians are also found on both sides of such public issues as

Military spending
The Equal Rights Amendment
Civil rights for homosexuals
Sex education in public schools
Busing for racial integration
Spraying herbicides
Nuclear energy
Abortion
School prayers
The teaching of evolution
Church involvement in politics

and such personal issues as

Moderate use of alcohol, tobacco, marijuana, coffee
Attending the theater
Playing cards
Watching television
Participating in sports or shopping on Sunday
Submission of women
Speaking in tongues

True, the Bible does give us many principles by which to discern right from wrong. Foremost among these are the

Lord's direct commands. As unequivocal as the Law seems, however, even some issues addressed in the Ten Commandments become more controversial the closer one examines them.

For example, the sixth commandment says, "Thou shalt not kill." Most evangelicals interpret this to mean "taking another's life in an act of personal malice." They would allow the killing of an enemy soldier as an act of war. They would permit killing a criminal against whom the state has issued a death sentence. And most approve killing animals for meat, for pelts, for nuisance control, and many even for sport.

"Obviously the commandment doesn't mean *that*," they would say. Nevertheless, some Christians feel it means exactly that. Which is my point: it isn't always so easy to know. Furthermore, it is not necessarily the person who is most sure of the matter who is closest to being right.

Jesus said to His disciples, "A time is coming when anyone who kills you will think he is offering a service to God" (John 16:2). Talk about confusing right with wrong. Think of it: people can commit heinous crimes and honestly feel virtuous about it!

Some Christians say that is what the United States did in Vietnam. Other Christians argue the contrary.

I think of three men with distinguished careers in the United States government: John Anderson, Mark Hatfield, and Jimmy Carter. Each is a confessed born-again Christian. Though all are Bible-believing Christians, they differ with one another on some major issues, and all of them have been far more liberal politically than many in their Christian constituencies.

Take Senator Hatfield, for instance. I cite him because we hail from the same state, Oregon, and I've followed his career for many years. Actions that Mark Hatfield calls for as an act of conscience (feeding disadvantaged nations rather than proliferating armaments), other Christians condemn as softness toward the godless enemy—Communist Russia.

Who is right? The point is, *right is not always easy to discern*. Following logically from that, the point is, further, that *sincere Christians may see things differently*. This implies, next, that *it is possible to be tragically wrong though sincere and firm in one's convictions*.

In light of the foregoing considerations, it follows that *we need to hold our positions with grace and humility, willing to change them if the facts require it*. Finally, a concomitant conclusion is that *we should accept and respect our brothers and sisters who disagree with us*.

I don't always agree with Mark Hatfield, and it is perfectly in order for me to challenge his positions or to question his arguments. What would not be in order would be to impugn the gentleman's character or Christian faith just because I disagree with his understanding of what Christian commitment requires in a certain situation.

Visitors to our state have asked me how Mark Hatfield continues to be elected since his positions are often contrary to those of many evangelicals in the state. My answer: he gets elected by an informal coalition of believers who do agree with him, believers who respect him even though they differ, and citizens who vote for him as the best candidate without reference to his religious beliefs.

Certainly some believers may feel they should pray that Senator Hatfield will grow in his ability to discern between right and wrong. Peter says that's something we *all* need to do. How can we add such knowledge?

First, as we observed a little earlier, one formidable roadblock to increased knowledge of any kind is the arrogant assumption that one already knows—or that at least he cannot learn from his "inferiors." This attitude is nothing but sinful pride and calls for repentance. Our prayer should be, "I'm sorry, Lord. Teach me Your will, and help me to be teachable."

This makes possible a second step: an honest inquiry into the facts. A person who really seeks the truth will consider both sides of a question. He will let the issues be debated freely. Instead of emotionally jumping the way his inclinations or prejudices lie, he will examine the merits of the respective claims. As the Bible says, "What a shame—yes, how stupid!—to decide before knowing the facts!" (Prov. 18:13, LB)

One should remember too that a middle position is possible on most issues, and that often the truth lies between two extremes. Maybe neither side is exactly right. Maybe neither is altogether wrong, either.

Third, we must practice making moral distinctions. Scripture teaches that discerning good and evil is a skill developed by use (Heb. 5:14). The easy way is to go along with the conventional wisdom. Many Christians do this without even knowing it. Because they belong to a group taking an adversary position to "the world," they imagine themselves to be nonconformists. Actually they may be conforming absolutely to their own group without ever questioning any of its positions.

We must use our powers of examination and discernment. This, plus studying the Word, are the ways to add authentic knowledge of good and evil to our characters. This knowledge could spare us from participating in some tragedies. I mean, surely we must avoid at all costs killing followers of Jesus while thinking we're doing God a service. Some mistakes are hard to fix.

6
Power to Do
What You
Want to Do

I recently conducted an admittedly unscientific survey on the subject of self-control. I called a number of friends and acquaintances, asking them to rate certain terms from 0-10, depending on whether the words evoked happy or unhappy feelings. They were not to compare each term with others on the list but with all possible words in the English language. That is, if a term was among the "happiest" of all possible words, it would rate a 10. If it was one of the "unhappiest" it would rate zero. The seven terms were *addict, diet, personal freedom, alarm clock, self-control, confidence,* and *achievement.*

My theory was that self-control has many negative associations in most people's minds and is not something viewed in a happy light. The results of the survey seemed to confirm this. The words in order of descending positive response, along with their averaged ratings, were:

achievement 9
personal freedom 8.67
confidence 8.5
self-control 6.5
alarm clock 4.5
diet 4.17
addict 1

Self-control came out significantly lower than the "happy" words on the list but significantly higher than the "unhappy" words. It seemed the respondents viewed self-control as including both happy and unhappy elements, for not only did it average in the mid-range, but each respondent placed it there. No one placed it at either extreme on the scale.

Who Needs It?

Popular literature about self-control is conspicuous by its absence. Only some 20 titles are listed under that broad subject title in *Books in Print*. Our local library, a pretty decent facility, catalogs no books on the subject.

The Bible, however, gives quite another picture. Though the term *self-control* is not found in the *King James Version*, Scripture actually says a good deal about it. What the *King James* calls *temperance*, most contemporary versions translate *self-control*. That's the situation where Peter admonishes us to add this trait to our faith (2 Peter 1:6). The same is true in Galatians (5:22-23), where Paul writes that self-control (temperance, KJV) is a fruit of the Spirit of God in our lives.

Centuries before Peter or Paul ever took pen in hand to exhort us to self-control, however, wise King Solomon wrote, "He that is slow to anger is better than the mighty, and he that ruleth his spirit than he that taketh a city" (Prov. 16:32, KJV).

When Alexander the Great burst on the world scene sometime later, he provided a living example of the truth of Solomon's words. Alexander took the "capturing of a city" to its ultimate by conquering the entire known world of his day. Yet because he could not rule his own spirit, he has gone down in history not only as a triumphant conqueror but also as a tragic figure. In a drunken rage, Alexander killed his own best friend, and he himself died at age 33, leaving behind the epitaph, "He conquered the world; himself he could not conquer."

Perhaps few people have the capacity for greatness Alexander had. Yet even he could not escape the destructive effects of a lack of self-control.

The Apostle Paul recognized that self-control is more critical to a person's true, lasting success than natural talent or power. He compared his own life to that of an athlete, who absolutely must embrace a rigorous training discipline if he is to be competitive.

Paul wrote:

> Everyone who competes in the games goes into strict training. They do it to get a crown of laurel that will not last; but we do it to get a crown that will last forever. Therefore . . . I beat my body and make it my slave so that after I have preached to others, I myself will not be disqualified for the prize (1 Cor. 9:25-27).

Self-Control or Self-Destruct

Why is self-control so vital? Is it because God doesn't want us to have any fun? Does He frown on spontaneity, on doing what comes naturally?

No, self-control is necessary because power of any kind becomes harmful when it is not carefully directed. I read the other day about a mechanical arm that went berserk. Seventy-five pounds of steel began slashing and slamming about, and woe unto anyone or anything that got in the way. Besides being a menace, the arm was also in danger of beating itself to pieces.

Behind the hydroelectric dams of the West, huge reservoirs store water which is used to generate the power that lights great cities and turns the wheels of vast industries. This is only possible because the water flow is controlled and directed through turbines. Should the dam burst and the water flow be uncontrolled, the resulting devastation would be awesome.

Millions on millions of people find the automobile to be a useful if not indispensable aid. But automobiles can and do wreak untold damage on property, besides killing and maiming thousands of people every year. What is the crucial factor that allows an invaluable aid to become a massive destroyer? Listen to the accident reports: "the vehicle went out of control," or "the driver lost control." These simple phrases tell it all.

We could multiply examples, but you get the point Think of virtually any kind of power and you have an example of a force which becomes destructive when it's not controlled.

The same holds true in our personal lives. That's why the Bible not only commands us to add self-control to faith but also tells us how we may do so. God wants our powers to serve, not destroy, ourselves and others.

What's Really Happening Here?

The very expression *self-control* is an interesting one. It raises the important question of who is controlling whom, or what is controlling what.

If you say to a person who is getting upset, "Control yourself," what are you actually recommending? And what are your underlying assumptions? It seems clear that you are assuming that the other person is a rational being who can be distinguished from his actions of the moment. He is not simply a reaction mechanism. At some deeper level of his being a *governor* resides. Someone is there. Someone who can select a different response to his stimulus than might naturally ensue.

By saying, "Control yourself," you are appealing to that inner governor. Self-control, then, involves establishing and strengthening the authority of your own inner governor. Therefore it should be seen as a wholly positive and liberating thing. It puts you in charge of your own life.

This view is quite in contrast with the unhappy assumption that self-control means a constricted lifestyle with no liberty to do what you want to do. This negative view is represented by an objectionable plaque I see occasionally. It reads, "Everything I like is either illegal, immoral, or fattening." I know that's supposed to be funny, but it betrays the attitude that self-control takes all the fun out of living.

The exact opposite is true. Self-control makes it possible to do what *you*, the inner person, want, rather than simply being driven by the passions that accompany your humanity.

Paul describes this well for the Christian: "For the sinful nature desires what is contrary to the Spirit, and the Spirit what is contrary to the sinful nature. They are in conflict with each other, so that you do not do what you want" (Gal. 5:17).

Notice carefully what Paul says happens to one caught in such a conflict: "You do not do *what you want*." Because of your uncontrolled desires, you are actually doing contrary to what the essential *you* wants to do.

For example, here's a woman with a weight problem. (It could as well be a man, but let's say it's a woman.) Does she want all the calories embodied in that chocolate éclair. No, she fervently wants a trim, healthy body. Obviously, something in her wants the éclair. Maybe it's her taste buds. Maybe it's her need to be loved. Maybe it's who knows what. The thing that's clear is that *she* doesn't want it, and she will feel terrible if she eats it.

Paul describes this kind of situation even more graphically in an oft-cited passage about "what I want to do I do not do, but what I hate I do" (Rom. 7:15). Clearly Paul's problem is not with his innermost desire but with his performance. "I have the desire to do what is good, but I cannot carry it out" (v. 18).

Often overlooked in this passage is Paul's observation about what all this reveals concerning him as a person. "Now if I do what I do not want to do, it is no longer I who do it, but it is sin living in me that does it" (v. 20).

Surely Paul doesn't say "it is no longer I" in order to excuse himself of responsibility. That clearly won't work. To say it is not "I" who overeats but "sin" in me certainly won't prevent me from getting fat, to stick with our eating example.

What is Paul's point then?

His point—and it's an important one—is that, as a person who knows and loves Jesus Christ, he delights in the Law of God in his innermost being (v. 22). He wants to live righteously. The sin in him is an intruder, a hostile alien.

To such a person, the self-control that can enable him to overcome sin and live righteously is altogether a positive thing. It is a glorious liberating power which makes it possible for him to more and more do what he wants to do instead of being enslaved by some bodily or emotional passion.

The joy of feeling one's life is under control, and the sense of dignity and well-being that brings, is far more valuable than any pleasures of self-indulgence.

Now, what about you? Perhaps you cannot say with Paul that "in my inner being I delight in God's Law." If that is the case, you are twice removed from wholeness. You have neither the deep desire nor the ability to keep God's Law. Nothing will do but for you to heartily turn to God for the forgiveness and grace which he bestows through faith in the Lord Jesus Christ. Then God's Law will be written in your heart, and you will be only once removed from a virtuous life. Then you will only need to add self-control to your faith.

7
Hope for the Weak-Willed

People tend to get discouraged easily in regard to self-control. They see it altogether as a matter of willpower, and since their willpower is somewhat deficient at best, they shrink from entering into any battles they feel likely to lose.

I have good news. There are ways to gain considerable self-control without necessarily having an iron will. If you've been defeated in this area of your life, consider how four self-control techniques that follow can work for you.

One of the few helpful reference works on self-control is *The Quest for Self-Control*, a collection of essays by 16 scholars, edited by Samuel Z. Klausner, published in 1965 by Macmillan. Klausner's own essay in this complex and difficult book reports on his study of 290 writings related to self-control. From this volumninous research, Klausner suggests four methods of self-control which he calls:

> the effort to synergy
> the effort to conquest
> the effort to harmony
> the effort to transcendance

I see a parallel between the methods Dr. Klausner suggests and the following four principles based on Scripture:

1. Control Yourself by Choosing Your Environment
When I was fresh out of high school, I wanted an education in

the Scriptures and enrolled at a Bible college. The small school I attended had rather relaxed academic standards, and I soon realized I could pretty much drift through—which I did. After one year, sensing I was not accomplishing anything, I transferred to a school with a reputation for tough study requirements. I lacked the willpower to make myself study consistently in the lax environment, but by choosing the stricter school I accomplished the same purpose.

This is but one example of the control-yourself-by-choosing-your-environment principle. Scripture speaks to this concept in many places and applies it to many of the situations that typically get people into trouble.

The principle has both a positive and a negative side. Putting myself into a strict school is an example of the positive—choosing an environment favorable to my purpose. Paul expressed the principle negatively: "Make not provision for the flesh, to fulfill the lusts thereof" (Rom. 13:14, KJV).

An application of the negative side? Well, a person unable to control salacious thoughts might better control some of the things that arouse such thoughts, such as the reading material perused or the shows watched.

In some cases one can seek self-control through both positive and negative environment control. For example, many people unable to discipline their eating habits by sheer willpower have done so through associations such as Weight Watchers and TOPS (Take Off Pounds Sensibly). The environment that is changed positively in such cases is one's associations. Support for weight control comes from the other members of the group.

Negative environmental change involves the banishing of fattening foods from kitchen shelves. One who lacks the willpower to resist a delicacy or junk food at hand might easily avoid purchasing such items in the first place.

Some Scriptures that reflect the self-control-through-a-helpful-environment principle are:

> He who walks with wise men will be wise,
> But the companion of fools will suffer harm
>
> (Prov. 13:20).

Do not associate with a man given to anger
or go with a hot-tempered man,
lest you learn his ways,
and find a snare for yourself

(Prov. 22:24-25).

When you pray, go into your room,
close the door,
and pray to your Father, who is unseen

(Matt. 6:6).

Let us not give up meeting together,
as some are in the habit of doing,
but let us encourage one another—
and all the more as you see the Day approaching

(Heb. 10:25).

An extreme form of environment control involves letting another person or an institution regulate one's entire life. This is usually appropriate only for small children. For adults it is extremely dangerous, and is typical of false cults. It is doubtful that one should ever enter such a relationship, but if it is occasionally warranted, it should always be temporary.

God never intended some of us to be satellite souls and others to lord it over His people, and we should say that loud and clear. Nevertheless, some wiped-out and incapacitated people, still children in character development and needing a great deal more guidance and correction than they can possibly provide for themselves, might temporarily need far-reaching external controls, but only in the process of developing their own self-control skills.

2. Control Yourself by Counteracting Bad Inclinations with Something Good

Here's how the Bible expresses this powerful principle: "Do not be overcome by evil, but overcome evil with good" (Rom. 12:21).

The grit-your-teeth-and-do-it-if-it-kills-you approach to self-control often misfires. The process is such an ordeal that it focuses your attention almost exclusively on the problem, when you probably need to turn your thoughts elsewhere. Even if you win a victory, it's such a costly one that next time you face the same battle you may feel it's not worth the struggle.

Someone has observed that one knows he has a drinking problem when he can think only about drinking, or about not drinking. The Bible says, "Do not get drunk on wine, which leads to debauchery. Instead, be filled with the Spirit" (Eph. 5:18). Notice that the Scripture here does not just declare a prohibition, but also gives an alternative. All the benefits drink may give—a feeling of freedom, release, good cheer, good will—can come through the filling of the Holy Spirit. And with no hangover, no liver or brain damage, and no menace on the road.

You cannot simultaneously use a given faculty to do good and evil. For example, you cannot speak the praises of God and complain or gossip or curse at the same time. If you have trouble controlling your tongue, and all of us do (see James 3:2-10), try substituting wholesome speech for evil:

words of thanks for complaints,
words of commendation for criticism,
words of praise for profanity,
words of interest in others for talk only of yourself.

If your problem is controlling your mind, don't just try to banish evil thoughts. Drive out the evil thoughts with good ones—by meditating on Scripture, for example.

The thought life is most critical in character building. The Bible specifically singles out our thoughts as an element of our lives that must be brought under control. "We take captive every thought to make it obedient to Christ" writes Paul (2 Cor. 10:5, see also Phil. 2:5; 4:8).

Your thought life is crucial because it is the seedbed of your actions and ultimately of your character. Probably you've heard this description of the relationship before:

Sow a thought; reap an action.
Sow an action; reap a habit.
Sow a habit; reap a character.
Sow a character; reap a destiny.

Everything begins at the level of your thoughts; they are the seeds of your subsequent actions, habits, and character.

The nature of the human mind is such that it must be occupied with something. We call people thoughtless and empty-headed when in fact they are quite busily thinking—of something other than what's appropriate at the time.

That's why, when it comes to thought-control, substituting something good for something evil is a dynamite principle, and probably the only effective technique one can use.

For example, thoughts of confidence in God are a powerful antidote to fear and worry. Instead of trying to tell yourself, "I won't be afraid," or "I won't worry," remind yourself how great and good and loving your heavenly Father is.

Observe, however, that this is far different from denying or repressing your fear and worry. To do that can make matters worse. If you try to ignore fear, it continues to lurk in the dark shadows of your mind, and can grow out of all proportion to the real threat it may represent. Instead of repressing your fear, put your hand in the hand of God and turn to face it. Often the fear will turn tail and run. And if not, you will at least see it as the limited threat it is, not the grotesque monster it seems to be.

Someone has written, "Fear came knocking on my door. Faith answered and found no one there."

That's good. The trouble is that sometimes when fear comes knocking at our door, we run and hide in the closet or make a lot of noise so we can't hear. But when we do, fear just knocks louder and louder.

Whether it's your speech, your thoughts, your spare time, or whatever, try counteracting your bad inclinations with something good. You'll get some amazing results.

3. Control Yourself by Meeting Your Legitimate Needs in Legitimate Ways

The Scripture applies this principle to sex by teaching that people with normal sexual drives ordinarily should marry. Then it says to the married couple, "Do not deprive each other [of sexual relations] . . . so that Satan will not tempt you because of your lack of self-control" (1 Cor. 7:5).

Some devout Christians have recorded sad experiences that resulted from violations of this principle. Assuming sexual activity to be base, or at least short of God's highest standards, they tried to live chaste lives. To their dismay, they found that the harder they tried to be pure, the more obsessed with sex they became and the more they struggled with sexual fantasies.

Generally it is God's will that natural sexual impulses be satisfied in natural marriage relations. No wonder there are self-control problems when people repress urges God put there in the first place and intended to be gratified.

Marriage is not a universal solution to the problem of sexual self-control. Not everyone who wants to be married is, and most people are single during part of their adult lives. Nevertheless, marriage remains a good example of self-control through meeting a legitimate need in a legitimate way.

The principle applies to more than sex, however. Any compulsive behavior (the kind you have difficulty controlling) likely stems from some unsatisfied basic need. Instead of simply trying to stop the behavior, search until you find the underlying need and find a God-honoring way to meet that need.

If you had to advise someone how to control a grumpy disposition and you knew the person was overwrought from lack of proper rest and diversion, what would you recommend? Would you say, "Be cheerful no matter how grim a task it is for you"? The contradiction in that advice should be obvious.

I would tell such a person, "It is senseless for you to work so hard from early morning until late at night, fearing you will starve to death, for God wants His loved ones to get their proper rest" (Ps. 127:2, LB). In other words, meet your legitimate needs in legitimate ways and you won't be so vulnerable to temptation.

4. Control Yourself by a Sheer Act of Will
We said that there are alternative ways to gain self-control, techniques not calling for great willpower. True, but there is

also a place for developing and using your will.

What often enters the picture here is not so much a lack of willpower as a lack of motivation. How many people have you known who tried to stop smoking and couldn't—until their doctor said quit or else? Suddenly they found the missing willpower.

We feel too sorry for ourselves. We know we should do this or that but it's "too hard." It doesn't take much of that sand in the gears to stop our engines cold. Whatever happened to "I can do everything through Him who gives me strength" (Phil. 4:13)

To say, "I should but I can't," is to speak against God. It implies that He requires more than I can deliver, that He is unjust. God will give us the power to do anything He commands us to do, if we depend on Him to do so.

Don't even think in terms of hard or easy, boring or interesting, dreary or exciting. Those descriptions are beside the point. What's needed is a plain and simple commitment to the will of God. Isn't that what living the Christian life is all about?

The Divine Plus

Do you realize that every self-control method suggested so far can be implemented by anyone, Christian or not? Rigidly self-controlled societies have existed in the past without Christianity. Remember the story about the little boy in ancient Sparta who, having hidden a fox in his tunic, never even winced as it bit into his chest until he fell down dead?

Though anyone can develop self-control, the Christian nevertheless has resources he did not have before he came to Christ. The Holy Spirit indwells the Christian, and one fruit of His presence and influence within us is self-control (Gal. 5:22-23).

The Holy Spirit also leads us into truth so that self-control does not get distorted into the warped, destructive thing it sometimes becomes in the world, as with the Spartan boy and the fox.

But how do we avail ourselves of this Holy Spirit power? By doing what Jesus told His disciples to do. "Watch and pray so that you will not fall into temptation. The Spirit is willing, but the body is weak" (Matt. 26:41).

See, Jesus knows we are weak. But He still tells us we will not fall if we'll *watch* (for temptation's approach) and pray (for the Spirit's strength).

Remember, we have this promise:

> God is faithful; He will not let you be tempted
> beyond what you can bear. But when you are tempted,
> He will also provide a way out so that you can stand
> up under it (1 Cor. 10:13).

So add self-control to your faith.

8
Why People Give Up

Thomas Edison, the great inventor to whom we owe a debt every time we switch on our electric lights, conducted some 18,000 experiments before he achieved that goal.

Dr. Jonas Salk of polio vaccine fame worked doggedly for three long years before he succeeded in blessing the world with an effective weapon against that crippling disease.

Abraham Lincoln, one of the greatest American Presidents, failed in tries for political office six times along the way to becoming President. (But, to keep the record straight, Abe also won six times during these same years.)

Albert Einstein, considered by many the greatest genius of the 20th century, said, "I think and think for months, for years; 99 times the conclusion is false. The hundredth time, I am right."

However gifted these men were, one thing becomes apparent. They would never have realized their potential without the character quality we call perseverance.

It is that quality of perseverance, plus a bit more, that we are next admonished to add to our faith as we build Christian character. Actually, it's difficult to come up with an expression that adequately conveys what is meant when Peter writes that we are to add "patience" to our faith (2 Peter 1:6, KJV). *Patience* is not a good translation, and few recent versions have retained it.

The problem is that *patience*, to most people, has come to mean virtually the opposite of irritability. It's what we need to control ourselves when the kids are acting up in the back seat of the car—*again*. Or it's that hard-to-come-by calmness one needs to tie a knot in a wispy strand of leader while icy dawn is breaking on a stream strongly suspected of hiding the wily steelhead.

Patience, in the biblical sense of a character trait each of us needs to cultivate, means much, much more than that. Two words commonly used to translate the original Greek *hupomone* (literally, "abiding under") are *endurance* and *perseverance*. Neither is a complete equivalent. The character trait we need embraces both of these qualities, as the two terms do convey somewhat different meanings.

Let's consider what endurance and perseverance are so that we may gain some understanding of *hupomone*.

Endurance is basically a passive trait. Something difficult is happening to you, but you are not being overwhelmed by it. For example, James writes, "Blessed is the man that endureth temptation, for when he is tried, he shall receive the crown of life" (James 1:12, KJV). When James speaks of enduring temptation, he views it as something that comes upon a person, something that happens to him. Endurance is his ability to withstand.

The writer of Hebrews gives another example. He writes that Jesus "for the joy set before Him endured the cross" (Heb. 12:2). Crucifixion was something that happened to Jesus, though He laid His life down willingly.

This is part of what the Lord is telling us to develop as a character trait, then—the ability to survive adversity, to "take a licking and keep on ticking."

But there is more. Perseverance is basically an active trait. One is doing something and encounters difficulty in continuing it or in seeing it through to a conclusion, but he sticks with the task. This "positive patience" is expressed in Scripture such as:

Let us not become weary in doing good, for at the proper time we will reap a harvest if we do not give up (Gal. 6:9).

Therefore, my dear brothers, stand firm. Let nothing move you. Always give yourselves fully to the work of the Lord, because you know that your labor in the Lord is not in vain (1 Cor. 15:58).

ages have collapsed because the people involved became
sioned, no longer believing that their situations were
le or desirable?

is brings us to a critically important question. What is one
who feels honestly disillusioned? Maybe the endeavor
y is not feasible. Does one go on beating his head against a
just so he can say he has perseverance? No, to do so is to be
ishly stubborn, and the result would likely be a concussion
he brain, not a change in the wall.

Ordinarily, those who speak for perseverance ignore this
ther side" of the question. For example, a popular poem by
dgar A. Guest reads:

> Somebody said that it couldn't be done,
>   But he with a chuckle replied
> That "maybe it couldn't" but he would be one
>   who wouldn't say so till he'd tried.
> So he buckled right in with the trace of a grin
>   On his face; if he worried he hid it.
> He started to sing as he tackled the thing
>   That couldn't be done, and he did it.

That's good. Quite inspirational. But let me suggest another,
less poetic, version:

> Somebody said that it couldn't be done. . . .
>   And sure enough, it couldn't!

I mean, some undertakings are virtually impossible. Perseverance is no doubt a wonderful virtue, but it won't do much
for a person trying to grow orange trees in the state of Maine.

A stubborn bloke may be disposed to argue the case, to claim
that walls can be battered down by the heads of persons skilled
in karate, that oranges can be grown in Maine greenhouses.
Perseverance would prevail even in these cases, it may be
claimed.

But such talk is beside the point. What may be remotely
possible is still not necessarily feasible. The question is, where
do we draw the line between perseverance and foolish
stubbornness? The answer: If the endeavor is in the will of
God, we should persevere against all odds, saying, "If God is
for us, who can be against us?" (Rom. 8:31) If it is not God's

The second dimension of this character trait, then, is the
ability to advance against opposition, to "fight the good fight" of
faith.

What term can we use to embrace both of these important
traits? Shall we settle for *patience*? Shall we use a descriptive
phrase such as *steadfast continuance*? Or use Williams'
translation, *"patient endurance"*? Perhaps we should coin a
word and call it *persedurance*, but who would know what we
meant? I guess we'll use whatever term—perseverance,
endurance, or steadfastness—seems to fit best at the time,
while remembering that we're talking about a single trait of
character, *the ability to keep on keeping on*.

Seven Threats to Perseverance

The Book of Hebrews is virtually centered on the theme of
perseverance. More than any other book in the Bible, it is
specifically written to encourage steadfastness in the fai.. .
survey of Hebrews uncovers many of the underlying problems
that cause people to give up. Correspondingly, seven secrets of
steadfastness are also suggested to us. Let's consider the
threats in the order in which they appear.

1. DEADLY DRIFT. "We must pay more careful attention,
therefore, to what we have heard, so that we do not drift away"
(Heb. 2:1). There is nothing dramatic here, no great collapse
occurring because of some secret sin or hidden weakness.
Instead, this danger first cited in Hebrews is a subtle one. People
fail to persevere simply because they lose interest. They become
inattentive, lethargic, careless, and they slowly drift away.

It's shocking to think that something as dynamic as *Christ in
you* can become ho-hum, but that's certainly what this warning
suggests. Didn't Jesus imply the same thing, though, when He
rebuked the church at Laodicea because they were lukewarm?
(Rev. 3:14-19)

T.S. Eliot suggested that the world will not end in a bang but
in a whimper. Just so, Scripture warns that your faith may not
fail in a crash but in a slow, perhaps imperceptible, drifting
away from God.

Like the other insights we may gain from the Hebrews letter, this principle may be applied both to one's Christian faith and to "secular" aspects of life. We begin a project either with great interest and enthusiasm or with the definite feeling that this is something we should do. After a time, however, the initial excitement or conviction wanes. We find the activity is like a hot bath: it doesn't seem so hot after we've been in it a while.

We also realize there's a price to pay. There are only so many hours in a day, and the fact that we are involved with this project keeps us from other things that look attractive. The first thing we know, we've quit for all practical purposes though we may continue to play around with the thing for a while longer to deceive ourselves and others about what is happening.

The remedy? "We must pay more careful attention . . . to what we have heard" (Heb. 2:1). What got us involved in the first place? If your project was valid at the time—and certainly in the case of Christian faith it was—it is probably just as valid now.

Let's apply the principle to see how it works.

Leroy began jogging because he heard of its fantastic benefits. Hardly anything would be better for his heart and lungs. Besides, he'd keep trim, generally feel better, and might even come to enjoy the jogging itself as a refreshing emotional/spiritual experience.

Leroy didn't hear all of this just once. It came from several sources including his friend Mike, whom Leroy believed implicitly. He was sure the claims were true.

So Leroy decided. He dug out an old sweat shirt and some tennis shoes and started jogging. Of course, he didn't expect fantastic results overnight. He wasn't that naive. This would take time. Meanwhile he decided he really should be properly equipped—good jogging shoes at least, and probably a jogging suit.

Now it's one year later. Leroy's jogging suit hasn't been out of the closet in six months and his wife is threatening to give it to the Salvation Army. What's the problem? Leroy has drifted

away. The facts that moved him in the [...] but he no longer pays attention to t[...]

What about you? Does deadly drif[...] intentions? Then face it. You decide. W[...] you began? Or were you right then an[...] away? If it's the latter, review "what[...] beginning till once again you are motivate[...] that reselling job as often as necessary to ke[...] you slip for a while. Or especially then. [...]

The first secret of steadfastness then is: *M[...] keep going by frequently reviewing the rea[...]*

Let's suppose you do this and it doesn't w[...] you had for beginning don't seem so importa[...] OK, you may be into perseverance problem[...]

2. DISILLUSIONMENT. "See to it, brothers, that [...] a sinful, unbelieving heart that turns away from t[...] . . . We have come to share in Christ if we hold [...] end the confidence that we had at first" (Heb. [...]

Much of the content of Hebrews is devoted to [...] how superior Christ is to the angels (chap. 1), to M[...] 3), and to the Levitical priesthood (chaps. 4, 7-10). T[...] there was no reason for these Hebrew believe[...] disillusioned with Christ. He was all they had ever [...] Him to be and infinitely more. The only basis [...] disillusionment on their part was unbelief—the idea th[...] had been sold a bill of goods and that Christ wasn't s[...] after all.

The writer to the Hebrews realized how utterly devast[...] to perseverance such disillusionment could be, and inc[...] must be. That is why he went to such lengths to reassure t[...] faith.

Disillusionment is extremely destructive to perseverance [...] whatever area of life it may occur. How many people hav[...] embarked on some weight-loss program—or on one afte[...] another—only to give up because the results were not what [...] they had hoped? How many small businesses have gone under, [...] how many projects have been abandoned, how many

will, we need to beware lest we be found beating our heads against a wall.

However, though distinguishing God's will in a clear good-versus-evil situation may be easy, how does a struggling businessman know whether to persevere or to sell? How does a person defeated in a bid for public office know whether to try again or to redirect his efforts? How does one who has failed a professional examination know whether to keep trying? How do I know whether or how long to keep broadcasting our Bible study program, *Truth for Our Times,* on a station that doesn't carry itself expense wise? In all these situations and many more, wise perseverance depends on knowing God's will.

It's no accident, then, that one of the key passages in Scripture dealing with perseverance also answers this will-of-God question.

> Consider it pure joy, my brothers, whenever you face trials of many kinds, because you know that the testing of your faith develops perseverance. Perseverance must finish its work so that you may be mature and complete, not lacking anything. *If any of you lacks wisdom, he should ask God,* who gives generously to all without finding fault, and it will be given to him (James 1:2-5).

The second secret of steadfastness, then, is to *develop a conviction through prayer as to what God's will for you is.*

Now, suppose you keep in mind all the reasons you have for doing this thing (so you won't drift), and you believe you are acting in the will of God (you aren't disillusioned), but nothing seems to be happening. You are discouraged and are facing the third threat to perseverance:

3. STALEMATE. "Therefore let us leave the elementary teachings about Christ and go on to maturity" (Heb. 6:1). The Christian life is intended to be one of continual growth and progress. "Let us go on" is its theme. The Christian who is stuck on dead center, at a stalemate, is also a Christian in great danger. For he who does not go on is likely to go back.

Similarly, few words are more discouraging in any enterprise than "no progress." Who wants to mark time, to see no results for his efforts? People are generally attracted to "where the action is" but are bored with static situations.

However, that's the whole point of perseverance. We are to continue in the face of discouragement, opposition, or seeming stalemate. How are we to resolve this dilemma? On the one hand we need to see progress so we won't give up, but on the other hand we must refuse to give up in order to see progress ultimately.

Enter *faith*.

Hebrews makes a major point of the principle that faith sees realities that are to be, not just those already realized. "Now faith is being sure of what we hope for and certain of what we do not see" (Heb. 11:1). In the rest of Hebrews 11, the writer cites stirring examples of this visionary quality of faith and then asserts, "All these people were still living by faith when they died. They did not receive the things promised; they only saw them and welcomed them from a distance" (v. 13). Not that they were defrauded in not receiving the things promised, but that their ultimate goals involved many generations and even reached into the next life.

The third secret of steadfastness is to *envision by faith the end result and believe you are inexorably moving toward that goal,* whether progress happens to be apparent right now or not.

Now, you are keeping in mind your reasons for acting, you have genuine conviction that this is the will of God for you, and by faith you see yourself moving toward the goal. What else is necessary? One thing is absolutely indispensable: *action*. Otherwise you can still be defeated by the fourth threat to perseverance:

4. LAZINESS. "We want each of you to show this same diligence to the very end, in order to make your hope sure. We do not want you to become lazy, but to imitate those who through faith and patience inherit what has been promised" (Heb. 6:11-12).

We don't hear much about laziness. It's such an unglamorous sin. There's no romance to it, no allure, no verve.

Preachers can't work up much thunder in denouncing it, and one would hardly guess it was one of the traditional seven deadly sins. The Bible, however, warns against sloth or indolence or laziness quite often, as in this passage: "We want each of you to show . . . diligence. . . . We do not want you to become lazy" (Heb. 6:11-12).

We might be in for quite a surprise if we could see how much and how often laziness is at the root of our spiritual difficulties. God's will is hindered because we are:

too lazy to search the Scriptures,
too lazy to pray through a matter,
too lazy to grasp our opportunities to help others,
too lazy to equip ourselves for greater service,
too lazy to write letters, phone people, communicate.

How often is our lack of perseverance attributable to plain ordinary laziness?

Laziness affects our lives much as inertia affects the physical world. The law of inertia in physics states that "matter remains at rest or in uniform motion in the same straight line unless acted upon by some external force." That is, an object at rest will remain so unless something makes it move, and a moving object will continue unless something makes it stop.

We human beings are somewhat like that. Why do you suppose it is harder to go back to the daily grind after a holiday or vacation? Inertia makes getting started the hardest part.

The inertia-like quality of laziness offers hope as well as danger, however. Why? Because it means that once you have stirred yourself to activity, it is not nearly so hard to continue.

Surely you have found this to be true. It was hard to start praying (or studying or working) but once you were under way it wasn't so unpleasant. You may even have enjoyed it.

Since perseverance by its very nature requires continuing action over a period of time, laziness is a serious threat that must be overcome. The fourth secret of steadfastness, then, is to make inertia work for you by forcing yourself to *take some small action toward your goal regularly*.

It's little short of amazing how much you will accomplish if you keep plugging away over a period of time, even though your progress seems agonizingly slow at times.

We'll consider the final three secrets of steadfastness in the next chapter. After all, we want this material to teach you endurance, not to be a test of it.

9
Seven Secrets
of Steadfastness

Isaac Watts wrote many of our greatest hymns, including "When I Survey the Wondrous Cross" and "Jesus Shall Reign Where'er the Sun." As a boy, he was so enchanted with rhymes that he used them in everyday speech. One day his father, impatient with the incessant verse coming out of little Isaac, told him to stop talking that way or to expect a spanking.

When Isaac failed to heed his father's warning, Mr. Watts turned the lad over his knee. Isaac, all apologies, cried, "O father, do some pity take, and I will no more verses make!"

Like Isaac, children often seem to have more perseverance "by accident" than their elders do on purpose. If they didn't, children would probably never learn to walk or talk.

But while children may have an edge on us adults when it comes to spontaneous perseverance, we surely have more capacity to apply sound principles that will produce perseverance in us as a character trait.

In chapter 8 we suggested four such principles corresponding to the four threats to perseverance:

1. DRIFT
2. DISILLUSIONMENT
3. STALEMATE
4. LAZINESS

We are ready now to consider three more threats to perseverance and three more secrets of steadfastness:

5. ISOLATION. "Since we are surrounded by such a great cloud of witnesses, let us . . . run with perseverance the race marked out for us. Let us fix our eyes on Jesus . . . who for the joy set before Him endured the cross. . . . Consider Him who endured such opposition from sinful men, so that you will not grow weary and lose heart" (Heb. 12:1-3).

If we had not realized before that the Book of Hebrews talks about endurance or perseverance, we should grasp the idea here. It's mentioned three times in these three verses.

Let's notice, first, how this passage again points up our number 3 secret of steadfastness: *envision by faith the end result and believe you are steadily moving toward that goal*. We are told here that Jesus faced the cross that way. "For the joy set before Him" He endured. His goal was to redeem us, and He focused on that, not on the terrifying obstacle that stood between Him and His goal.

The second thing we need to notice about our efforts to endure is that we are not supposed to go it alone. All the faithful Christians who have gone before us demonstrated by their lives that believers—we as well as they—can endure virtually anything. We should draw on their example for inspiration.

We also have Christian brothers and sisters today in whom we see real courage under trial, as well as those who stand by to help us if they can, or just stand by when no more can be done. We should thank God for such people and pray that their tribe may increase and that more and more believers might show they care whether others make it or not, whether in the Christian life, on the job, with their families, or wherever.

So far as our perseverance is concerned, there are even people outside the church who can help us. There are support groups for alcoholics and the families of alcoholics, for drug abusers and the families of drug abusers, for the overweights and the underprivileged, for the single and the divorced. Indeed there are support groups for almost every special interest. No one has to struggle on alone.

Even worse than trying to endure without the help of other people, however, is neglecting the help of the Lord Himself. Examine the life of anyone who has overcome great obstacles, and you will most likely find a person who has drawn strength from the Lord.

Moses "persevered because he saw Him who was invisible" (Heb. 11:27).

David wrote, "I have set the Lord continually before me; because He is at my right hand I will not be shaken" (Ps. 16:8).

Paul wrote, "I can do everything through Him who gives me strength" (Phil. 4:13).

Christ is more than the supreme example of endurance. He is a direct source of strength, One from whom we "may receive mercy and find grace to help us in our time of need" (Heb. 4:16).

So when you feel discouraged, beaten—or perhaps worse, indifferent—don't give up and don't struggle on alone. Reach out to Jesus. He will be there, and He will restore your soul. "Those who wait for the Lord will gain new strength; they will mount up with wings like eagles; they will run and not get tired; they will walk and not become weary" (Isa. 40:31). What a beautiful description of perseverance this is!

So the fifth secret of perseverance is: don't try to go it alone, but *draw help from the Lord and from people He has prepared for that purpose.*

The sixth threat to perseverance is perhaps the most damaging of all:

6. SELF-PITY. "In your struggle against sin, you have not yet resisted to the point of shedding your blood" (Heb. 12:4). The Hebrews thought their lives were tough, and to a degree they were. They had been persecuted and had suffered material loss. Still those believers were not actually being killed or tortured.

The point is that "poor me" is not an attitude calculated to produce endurance. It's much more likely to lead to "I want out."

Few worthwhile things can be accomplished without suffering. But if one focuses his attention on the suffering, he will lead an unhappy life at best and will likely become a quitter.

Paul suffered for the faith, probably far more than any of us, but what was his attitude toward it? "I consider that our present sufferings are not worth comparing with the glory that will be revealed in us" (Rom. 8:18). His complete lack of self-pity played a big part in enabling Paul later to rejoice in the fruits of his perseverance. He could say, "I have fought the good fight, I have finished the race, I have kept the faith" (2 Tim. 4:7).

There is a hidden element here that we must not overlook. Self-pity thrives on unrealistic expectations. We must therefore factor suffering into our plans in a realistic manner.

Jesus said, "Suppose one of you wants to build a tower. Will he not first sit down and estimate the cost to see if he has enough money to complete it?" (Luke 14:28)

My friend and neighbor Don Michael is a builder who knows from experience what expenses to anticipate in constructing a home. Nevertheless, included in his estimates is a sum for something called "contingency." That is to provide for expenses Don doesn't foresee, though he is expert at foreseeing them all.

Mark it down. Whatever the undertaking, you should expect unexpected costs. Then when they come, you will not be overwhelmed. Instead of saying, "Poor me, this is so hard," you will say, "Well, I never expected this to be easy, and I see I was right!"

The Bible records many cases of heroic perseverance. Few are more inspiring than the three young Hebrews who persevered in refusing to worship the golden image set up by King Nebuchadnezzar of Babylon.

When the three men were called to account before the king and told to worship the king's image or die by fire, they did not buckle. Their reply to the king is significant. "Our God whom we serve is able to deliver us from the furnace of blazing fire, and He will deliver us out of your hand, O King. But even if He does not, let it be known to you, O King, that we are not going to serve your gods" (Dan. 3:17-18).

Note that "but even if He does not" part. That's the contingency clause. That's counting the cost in a realistic manner. The Hebrew youths persevered because, going in, they took into account the worst eventuality and were prepared for it.

Jesus also spoke to this theme in a parable about different kinds of people who hear the Word of God. One type "hears the Word and at once receives it with joy. But since he has no root, he lasts only a short time. When trouble or persecution comes because of the Word, he quickly falls away" (Matt. 13:20-21).

Jesus was describing a person who does not persevere, who "lasts only a short time." And why? Because his commitment is superficial. He has not counted the cost and is not prepared to cope with difficulty. With him, it's easy in and easy out.

The sixth secret of steadfastness, then, is to *pursue your endeavor with a realistic appraisal of the difficulties to be expected*. This will enable you to take them in stride when they arise.

One more threat to perseverance remains:

7. MISJUDGING GOD. "Endure hardship as discipline; God is treating you as sons. For what son is not disciplined by his father?" (Heb. 12:7)

When the writer to the Hebrews says to "endure hardship as discipline," he is telling us what attitude we should have. He is teaching us how to view the difficulties that come into our lives.

How do you usually look on your difficulties?

I'm afraid that too often I react with anger. When things don't go right for me, I tend to get quite upset. A recent episode leaps to mind. I'm constructing a pole building on the small acreage I mentioned earlier. In the process, I'm meeting the usual quota of difficulties, but that's been no special problem because I applied steadfastness secret number 6: *pursue your endeavor with a realistic appraisal of the difficulties to be expected*.

One day not long ago, I was ready to quit at 4:30 P.M. so that I could get to a 6:30 dinner meeting where I was scheduled to speak. My final task for the day was to move a trailer load of two-by-fours a few hundred feet to the building site, where I would simply unhitch the trailer and head for home, half a mile away. A two-minute task. Nothing to it. What could possibly go wrong?

Well, the car started normally and ran fine till I got the trailer load of lumber right smack in the middle of the narrow lane, and then it died. It stubbornly refused to start again. I might cheerfully have abandoned the whole rig for the time being (I had ample time to walk home and still make the meeting on time), but I couldn't leave the disabled car in the drive since that was the only way the people beyond had for getting to and from their home.

There was nothing to do but jog home, get another car and a tow chain, and go drag the offending equipment off the road into the ditch. Which is what I did, but not, I'm afraid, with good humor.

I made the meeting on time, and thanks to God's graciousness, everything there went well. No doubt I could have reacted to that trial in a better way—and suffered less emotional wear and tear in the process. My anger subsided quickly, however, and it was no real threat to my perseverance.

Anger, then, is bad enough, but other reactions to difficulty can be much worse. Discouragement is the reaction against which we are specifically warned. "Do not lose heart when He rebukes you" (Heb. 12:5).

When we lose heart, we have also misjudged God. In permitting difficulties to beset us, He "disciplines us for our good, that we may share in His holiness" (v. 10). He isn't seeking to thwart our good efforts. He isn't toying with us. And He certainly is not sadistically giving us a hard time for the fun of it.

I have fleeting moments when, frustrated at every turn, I say, "Well, I might just as well go sit and watch television all day for all I'm accomplishing." But I don't mean it, and I certainly don't do it. I may take a break or turn to some other constructive endeavor for a time, but because I know God wants me to engage in life's struggle for a twofold reason, I go on. What is the twofold reason? To *produce* something good and to *become* something good. I must never lose sight of those goals—and especially of the second one when the first seems thwarted.

God's Word says, "Make every effort to add to your faith . . . perseverance" (2 Peter 1:5-6). You can do so by putting to work the insights you have now gained. To the faltering projects in your life, and to those being contemplated, apply the seven secrets of steadfastness:

1. Review the reasons you have to do this thing.
2. Pray until conviction comes of God's will for you.
3. See yourself as moving steadily toward your goal.
4. Take some small step toward your goal regularly.
5. Avail yourself of timely help from others and especially from the Lord.
6. Pursue your endeavor with a realistic expectation of the difficulties.
7. Believe that God will make you a better person through your struggles as you persevere.

10
Making Your Character Truly Christian

Dad Iverson is 81 years old now. He worked in the South Dakota gold mines for a while way back when the girl who was to become my wife was born. Most of his life, he was a Washington State farmer. The last few years of his working life were spent in a hospital laundry.

Dad always worked hard, was faithful to his wife, and raised eight children. For many years he was the chief support of the country Sunday School where he lived, and he is still active in church to this day.

Recently I asked him, "If you had it all to do over again, what would you do differently?"

He didn't have to think about it. "I'd be a missionary," he answered at once.

Now, mind you, Dad did not neglect a missionary call early in life. He didn't even become a Christian until he was in his forties, with a wife and seven children.

But almost from the time of his conversion, Dad bought into the notion that if he were really to do the will of God it would mean selling out everything and becoming a missionary. Since that wasn't feasible, he didn't see how he could truly be the Christian he should be. And with that attitude, he wasn't. Oh, he lived as good a Christian life as the next church member—probably better than most, but he didn't live as close to God as he would have if it hadn't been for the guilt and the feeling, "Well, I'm not really what I ought to be anyhow, so what's the difference?"

Now, here I am writing about godliness, Peter's fifth-listed character trait, and scared to death of doing more harm than good. I must not lower God's standards to make godliness cheap and easy. But neither must I discourage and defeat God's people by falsely making it seem hard.

Let me try to be completely honest. I think that much the greater temptation for me is to make godliness seem harder than it is. Why? Because if I don't, my critics can find fault with me. They can say that I'm not godly myself so naturally I don't require much. On the other hand, if I tell my readers they ought to pray three hours a day (early in the morning, without fail), study God's Word another three hours, and spend the rest of their time witnessing, I'd sound truly "spiritual."

However, I'd also be laying on my brothers and sisters a burden which no one in the real world is able to bear—with a few exceptions possibly, but even those people's superior sanctity is open to question. An old poem says it well:

The parish priest, of austerity,
　　Climbed up in a high church steeple,
To be nearer God, so that he might hand
　　His Word down to the people.

And now and again when he heard the crank
　　Of the weathervane a-turning,
He closed his eyes and said, "Of a truth,
　　From God I now am learning."

In sermon script he daily wrote
　　What he thought was sent from heaven,
And he dropped this down on his people's heads
　　Two times, one day in seven.

In his age God said, "Come down and die!"
　　And he cried out from the steeple,
"Where art Thou, Lord?" And the Lord replied,
　　"Down here among My people."

It's true. God does dwell in the midst of His people, and the godly person is not one who seeks somehow to resign from the human race and just meditate.

With this in mind, I'll risk the critics' scorn and resist the temptation to make high-sounding pious demands of the reader. At the same time, I must not merit criticism by going to the other extreme and embracing an activism that neglects devotion.

I ask then, why must we complicate the Christian life so? Centuries ago, the Prophet Micah swept aside all the confusion and set forth the essence of godliness: "He has told you, O man, what is good; and what does the Lord require of you but to do justice, to love kindness, and to walk humbly with your God?" (Micah 6:8)

Oh, if Dad Iverson could only have grasped years ago the liberating message of those words! Why, he *did* those things. Not perfectly of course, but he treated people fairly and kindly, and walked humbly with God. But he thought godliness was something far beyond the reach of an ordinary man; it meant being a missionary.

Starting Over

It's odd the way we think about godliness. Most of us would shrink from claiming we have it. Yet we would be highly insulted if we were called *un*godly. To understand what godliness actually is, let's ponder it together, asking the Holy Spirit to lead us into truth.

The Greek term translated godliness literally means to be "well devout." W.E. Vine calls it "that piety which characterized by a Godward attitude, does that which is well-pleasing to Him." I like Micah's phrase better: to "walk humbly with your God."

I would suggest that godliness, at a minimum requires three elements clearly set forth in Scripture:
- Recognition of God
- Awareness of God
- Devotion to God

1. Recognition of God

Now, as through the ages past, the secular mind is strangely ignorant of the presence of God. This is a mark of man's alienation. The Apostle John describes this situation quite graphically. Speaking of Christ the eternal Word, he writes, "He was in the world, and though the world was made through Him, the world *did not recognize Him*" (John 1:10).

It is true, as most people understand this passage, that the world did not recognize Jesus as the incarnation of the eternal Word. But the Apostle John says more than that. The failure to recognize God's presence is typical of man throughout his whole long history of alienation from God.

From the very beginning, God's Son was present in the world, animating man, enlightening him, inspiring him, appealing to him. John writes, "In Him was life, and that life was the light of men. The light shines in the darkness, but the darkness has not understood it" (John 1:4-5).

Do you see what John is saying? The life of God is the source of all man's enlightenment, but man has not understood that. Even now, many Christians don't understand it. God gives some wisdom and insight to atheists as well as to Christians. He is the source of all truth, not just "spiritual" truth. That is why John declares Christ to be "the true light that gives light *to every man*" (John 1:9).

The first element of godliness is to recognize God as Creator/Originator/Sustainer/Enlightener. As the psalmist expressed it, "Know that the Lord Himself is God; it is He who has made us, and not we ourselves; we are His people and the sheep of His pasture" (Ps. 100:3).

2. Awareness of God

It is one thing to recognize God and another to be aware of Him. To say that God is present everywhere is much different from sensing that He is *here, now*.

Jacob as a young man certainly recognized God. Indeed, it was that recognition which set him apart in his early years from his essentially secular twin brother Esau. Jacob valued the spiritual dimension, the Godward aspect of life, while Esau did not. That was why Jacob schemed to buy and Esau consented to sell the birthright, a transaction that marked both boys for life.

Young Jacob, however, was not a godly person, for mere recognition of God is not enough. Observe Jacob a while and you will see he hasn't added godliness to his faith.

Jacob has left home, fleeing the wrath of Esau, who is ready to kill him for the outrageous dirty tricks he has pulled. This isn't exactly a well-planned trip on which Jacob is embarking and he has no motel reservations along the way. He stops for the night wherever he happens to be when it gets too dark to travel farther.

We find Jacob, then, sleeping on the ground, with nothing but a stone for a pillow. Not a soft resting place for his head, but enough prop to spare him a stiff neck in the morning.

We're told that while Jacob was sleeping in this manner, "he had a dream" (Gen. 28:12). I shouldn't wonder! I'd have dreamed too.

In Jacob's dream, God stood above the top of a ladder that reached into heaven. God spoke only good to Jacob—in fact, God promised him the same birthright blessings he had schemed and connived to get.

Then Jacob awoke. What would you expect his reaction to be? Joy, because his heart's desire was to be granted?

Not quite. "Then Jacob awoke from his sleep and said, 'Surely the Lord is in this place, and I did not know it.' And he was afraid and said, 'How awesome is this place! This is none other than the house of God, and this is the gate of heaven'" (Gen. 28:16-17).

How can we explain Jacob's fear, which seems so out of keeping with the good news God has just given him? Part of the answer lies in his guilt. God's presence is always threatening to guilty people. But beyond that, just to think that Almighty God is *there*. Notice Jacob's first comment: "Surely the Lord is in this place, and I did not know it."

Exactly! Those words well describe a believer who lacks

godliness. He is unaware of the presence of the Lord, who in fact is "in this place" wherever we are.

To be godly, then, you must develop an awareness of God. Wherever you may be, under whatever circumstances, realize that God is there. (Yes, even in the tough situation you face right now from which God seems most remote.)

How is one to develop this awareness of God so essential to a godly character? William Law in his classic book, *A Serious Call to a Devout and Holy Life* (first published in 1728), prescribes a five-times-daily prayer regimen. The first daily prayer time is to be early in the morning. Law writes:

> I take it for granted that every Christian that is in health is up early in the morning, for it is much more reasonable to suppose a person up early because he is a Christian than because he is a laborer, or a tradesman, or a servant, or has business that wants him.

Law makes it clear that praying whenever you would normally arise is not sufficient. When he says early, he means *early*. "It is as much your duty to rise to pray, as to pray when you are risen."

At 9 A.M. you are to be at prayer again, this time directing your prayers toward your need of humility.

The noon season of prayer should focus on love.

At your 3 P.M. prayers, you will resign yourself to the will of God.

Evening prayer is to be spent in self-examination, in specific confession of sin, and in cultivating "a just horror and dread of sin."

Who would criticize such a practice as Law prescribes? Not I. But I do question his imposing it on others. Like Dad Iverson's missionary imperative, it's a bit impractical for those facing the demands of living in today's western world. Most jobs probably would not permit such a practice, and that includes homemaking.

The ritual of praying five times daily is observed in Muslim countries, but short of moving to the Middle East, the question remains: How do we develop awareness of God while living in our world as it is?

More promising than the idea of a five-times-daily routine is the scriptural admonition to "pray continually" (1 Thes. 5:17). In other words, we should be constantly relating to God, as well as praying at whatever designated times God may lead us to establish.

I remember my first visit to the Wailing Wall, that remnant of Solomon's Temple, so sacred to Jews, in Jerusalem. Our Hebrew guide Joseph had us men don small black skull caps out of respect, he said, for Jewish belief that such should be worn there "in the presence of God." Some Jewish men, he explained, wore the caps all the time, believing they are always in the presence of God.

Exactly. We do not need to cap our heads, but we do need to cultivate an awareness of the divine Presence. That means we should awake with a "Thank You, Lord, for this new day" and a prayer that we might use it well. It means that all day long we should pray to God whenever we're in trouble and praise Him when we're not (James 5:13). And it means we should end the day by presenting ourselves before the Lord once again, perhaps for forgiveness, to commit the efforts of the day to Him, or simply to sink with exhaustion into His tender care just as our body sinks into the bed.

3. Devotion to God

The third element essential to godliness is a responsive heart. It is not enough to recognize God and to be aware of His presence if one's heart is indifferent or rebellious. Satan himself recognizes God and no doubt is fully aware of Him. Yet Satan is the antithesis of godliness because he is in a state of rebellion.

Jesus, by contrast, maintained a constant devotion to the will of His Father. "'My food,' said Jesus, 'is to do the will of Him who sent Me and to finish His work'" (John 4:34).

When we lose sight of God and His will, whether we're forgetting God or fighting Him, we cannot claim to be leading godly lives. We are not walking humbly with our God.

The three elements of godliness may be traced in the life of the boy Samuel. As he lay sleeping one night, he heard a voice calling him. Not recognizing the voice to be God's, Samuel responded by going to the bedside of Eli the priest. This happened three times before the aged Eli realized what was happening. He then told Samuel, "Go lie down, and it shall be if He calls you that you shall say, 'Speak, Lord, for Thy servant is listening'" (1 Sam. 3:9).

Samuel, now realizing whose voice he had heard, returned to his bed. We do not know how long he waited, but after some time he became aware of a presence. "'Samuel! Samuel!' And Samuel responded, 'Speak, for Thy servant is listening'" (v. 10).

Those words express the third essential element of godliness—a devotion to the Lord and a readiness to do His will.

Does "Thy servant is listening" describe your heart's attitude toward God? Are you responding to the Lord's Word? Are you seeking to walk with Him in a humble, teachable spirit? That is godliness. And if "Thy servant is listening" becomes characteristic of your life, you will, to a degree at least, have added godliness to your faith.

The Companions for Godliness

When I began to study the traits of Christian character, I had no intention of limiting myself to the list in 2 Peter 1:5-7, and no reason to do so. There are important character traits in Scripture that Peter does not mention, and we should also explore them.

At first it seemed Peter's list was certainly incomplete. Humility, gratitude, loyalty, and truthfulness were omitted, to name a few.

On further reflection, however, most if not all of the omitted traits seem to be included under those Peter mentioned. The first trait, goodness, is quite comprehensive and would certainly include truthfulness, for example. Loyalty is a form of perseverance combined with brotherly love. Humility and gratitude both relate directly to godliness.

Let's observe how godliness produces these other graces. The most powerful passage I think of in Scripture for the inculcation of humility is 1 Corinthians 4:7: "For who makes you different from anyone else? What do you have that you did not receive? And if you did receive it, why do you boast as though you did not?"

The passage reminds us that everything good we have is from God. This means we have much to be thankful for (a basis for gratitude), but nothing to be proud of (a basis for humility). Godliness, then (recognizing God, being aware of and devoted to Him), is inconsistent with both pride and ingratitude.

Another beautiful thing about godliness is that its inclusion makes character-building truly Christian, unlike the secular self-help programs currently abounding. Some of these programs undoubtedly help people, but they can also warp and distort one's personality by encouraging self-centeredness.

As Dr. Paul Vitz, associate professor of psychology at New York University, writes, "Psychology has become a religion, in particular, a form of secular humanism based on worship of the self."

Vitz comments further:

> Like all popular heresy, selfism has some positive and appealing properties. That you should look out for yourself is nice (and useful) to hear; that you should love and care for others is a familiar and great moral position. What is excluded is the spiritual life of prayer, meditation, and worship—the essential vertical dimension of Christianity, the relation to God.*

What Vitz says selfists exclude is emphatically included by the Apostle Peter when he urges us to add godliness to faith. A good strong dose of this "Peter's prescription" will save us from the sickness of a one-sided, self-help psychology.

Still Vitz makes quite a concession to popular psychology when he writes,

> Selfism is an example of a horizontal heresy, with its emphasis only on the present, and on self-centered ethics. At its very best (which is not often), it is Christianity without the first commandment.

---

*Psychology as Religion, the Cult of Self-Worship, Eerdmans.

What must God think as He looks down on the human race? It seems many of the well-meaning people on earth follow a horizontal heresy and many others a vertical heresy. Vitz has described the horizontal heresy: people leave godliness out of their lives of goodness. The vertical heresy is leaving goodness out of a life of godliness. It is behaving as if godliness were the only trait God's Word says to add to faith. It is being unconcerned about goodness, knowledge, self-control, perseverance, and brotherly kindness.

Take George, for instance. George is a "zealous Christian." He takes a strong stand against social evils of every kind. He has a Bible verse for almost every situation and sees as his chief purpose in life the conversion of others (to faith in Christ as Saviour *and* to all his views on "spiritual" matters).

George also does not hold a regular job. It might interfere with his "ministry" as a self-appointed evangelist. His wife is the principal breadwinner in the family. George beats his wife. It's his way of exacting the absolute submission from her that he says the Bible requires. He is generally so cruel and insensitive toward his wife that she has at times been near suicide.

George shows no inclination to add knowledge to his faith, but instead displays an arrogant bigotry. He is a vertical heretic.

But let's speak of better things. Do you know someone who possesses a hideous, distorted, one-sided, false godliness? For each such person, there are many more whose lives have been made beautiful by true godliness, which added to faith along with goodness, knowledge, self-control, perseverance, and brotherly kindness, has brought a balance that glorifies God and is useful to other people.

Lord, grace each of us with that kind of beauty.

11
The Touch that Helps and Heals

Frank was an active member of our church, a congenial fellow whom we all liked. He was a key leader of the men's fellowship, and was instrumental in that group's sponsoring a one-hour weekly Gospel music program on our local secular radio station. Often Frank hosted the program. Personally, I found his easy, down-home style appealing, in spite of the fact that he frequently fractured the king's English.

One Sunday at our church worship service, aired over the same station, Frank was scheduled to lead the congregation in the morning prayer. As he did so, he included at least two or three times the petition that God would bless every "faucet" of the ministry.

I knew Frank meant every "facet" of the work, but the mental image of a water faucet was amusing to me, and I still had a grin on my face when I looked up at his "Amen." Directly across from me, in the choir, my oldest daughter Kathy looked up at the same time, the same amused expression on her face.

Just as our eyes met, Frank turned from the pulpit and caught us grinning at each other. After the service, he asked me what we had found so funny. I had to tell him, though I tried my best to minimize it and to assure him I appreciated his participation in the service. Frank was offended and would never again lead in the morning prayer.

Now, I'll grant that I may have been slightly deficient in brotherly kindness. To laugh or even smile at a person who's not meaning to be funny can be cruel in its effect, though in this case it was certainly not so intended. Some readers may feel Frank was justified in refusing to pray publicly any more lest he subject himself to further "ridicule."

But the underlying principle in action here is a false and dangerous one, if Frank was saying by his attitude: *it's not worth it to participate and risk getting hurt*. Such a principle, followed consistently, would lead one into almost total withdrawal and isolation since slights, misunderstandings, and hurts inevitably occur when we interact with other people.

Philadelphia

Withdrawal from interaction with people runs directly counter to at least one character trait God wants us to develop. For God had Peter write, "Add to your faith . . . brotherly kindness" (2 Peter 1:5-7). The original Greek term here is *philadelphia*, which is usually translated "brotherly love."

Philadelphia implies a gregarious, people-loving attitude that sees the value, benefits, and just plain fun of relating to others as far outweighing the incidental hurts. You see, the love connoted by the word *phileo* involves tender affection. It is a more emotional word than *agape*, that divine love which esteems and values the object loved but doesn't necessarily feel affection. We might say that *agape* means loving others, but *phileo* means liking them, enjoying their company, intertwining our lives with theirs.

With this in mind, we need to think again about the claim sometimes heard that we must love people but we don't have to like them. This claim is especially off the mark if we use it to justify disliking nearly everyone. Such an attitude on our part reveals much more about us than it does about people we don't like. It reveals that we haven't added brotherly love to our faith.

Will Rogers is famous for having said, "I never met a man I didn't like." I doubt that tells you much about the people he

met during his lifetime. But it does tell you something about
Will Rogers.

The Balance

The further we penetrate into Peter's list of character traits,
the more remarkable we find it. The first four character
traits—goodness, knowledge, self-control, and perseverance—relate primarily inward to the self. Based on that fact,
we can say without hesitation that it is legitimate to work at
self-improvement. More than legitimate, since the Word
urges the self-improvement on us in the strongest terms. Our
personalities need these important qualities.

Nevertheless, in telling us what we should become, Peter
makes it clear that we can never be all we ought to be so long as
we are turned inward. Thus, as we saw in the previous chapter,
Peter directs us to other dimensions of life. In urging us to add
godliness, Peter is pointing us more upward than inward.
Besides being OK within (having the integrated personality of
which psychologists speak), we need to be OK toward God, to
add godliness to faith.

Now Peter directs us to yet another dimension for complete
personhood. Not inward, not upward—but outward. It is not
enough that we be OK within and OK toward God; we also
need to be OK toward other people. "Add to your faith . . .
brotherly kindness."

What all is involved in this matter of being rightly related to
other people? Obviously, a great deal. Volumes have been
written on this subject. We can touch only on a few high points,
and perhaps suggest fruitful sources for further inquiry.

The first requirement, already suggested, is that we do
relate. We must not disassociate ourselves. We must not
withdraw into isolation.

However, the way we relate is critically important as well. In
fact, Paul told the Christians at Corinth, "Ye come together not
for the better, but for the worse" (1 Cor. 11:17, KJV). Their
relationships were toxic, not edifying, and one reason for this
sad state was that they were so divided (see v. 18).

Love, Acceptance, and Forgiveness

Jerry Cook and I have written a book about the Lord's powerful solution to the terribly hurtful problem of divisiveness and other difficulties that injure Christians. The book is titled *Love, Acceptance, and Forgiveness*.* The following excerpt describes how Pastor Cook applies its principles:

> In 1978 I was away from my church for about three weeks to hold a pastors' conference in New Zealand. When I left home, the people at East Hill were concerned with loving one another and being filled with the Holy Spirit. I returned to find them upset, unhappy with one another, and jabbing at one another.
>
> The ladies' ministries had sponsored a fashion show. As a part of the fashion show, one of the women had modeled a bikini. The local newspaper covered the fashion show and along with their article ran one picture. You guessed it—a shot of the gal in the bikini. Some of the members were quite upset about this turn of events and were ripping into the model and the woman responsible for the fashion show.
>
> The bikini had been only a small part (no pun intended) of the fashion show, which in turn was only a part of the program that night. In fact, through the testimonies and that entire program presented to some 500 women, several of them gave their lives to Christ. The newspaper had presented a positive write-up, praising the fashion show as one of the finest. And the bikini photo had been published without comment.
>
> When all this landed in my lap on my return from New Zealand, I was upset. Not about the bikini. It's false to be upset about a bikini in a fashion show and not about the ones being worn at almost every swimming pool. Anyhow, only women were present and it would not have mattered to me if they had been modeling lingerie.
>
> I could see some reason for concern over the picture in the paper but I was a whole lot more concerned that Christians were ripping Christians, and a spirit of criticism was replacing a spirit of love, acceptance, and forgiveness.
>
> I met privately with the woman who had modeled the bikini and the woman who set up the fashion show. I said, "There has been some objection to the content as you know. Most of the complaints have come from men, none of whom were present. But maybe they have a point. Maybe you need to evaluate your

*© 1979, Regal Books, Ventura, CA 93003. Used by permission.

program, keeping in mind your weaker brothers. But no one is judging you. I'm backing you 100 percent, and that is what I'm telling those who come to me."

The women decided they would forego their rights and omit bikinis in the future; it was no big deal.

The more serious problem, the unloving criticism, called for action from me. I brought the whole situation out in the open in a service. I told the people that knowledge (in this case, knowledge of what should not be done and why) puffs up, but love builds up (1 Cor. 8:1). I told them that they were responding to this situation below the level of their maturity in Christ. Love won the day, the critics saw their error, and the fellowship was restored.

If the women had actually done something wrong, I'd still have taken action against any critical spirit developing. If something is wrong, we simply acknowledge that it's wrong and pray that the devil won't be able to seize on it as a means of hurting people. We don't abet the devil's work by making or promoting attacks on the people involved. We talk with them, deal with the issue, and treat them with love, acceptance, and forgiveness.

This same book contains much more valuable information on brotherly kindness, especially as it applies to church life.

What Did Jesus Say?

Further insight into what all is involved in brotherly love and kindness can be gained by considering the chapter titled "Relating to Others" from my book *What Did Jesus Say about That?** What Jesus said, most emphatically, was that the second greatest commandment of all is to love our neighbors as ourselves, that is, to add brotherly love to our faith.

As the book points out, however:

Our love for one another often doesn't stand a chance. Other dynamics are operating so strongly that love is crowded from the scene. For example, we are often too busy resenting people to love them.

The book goes on to suggest several scriptural ways to resolve resentment. Then it zeroes in on two other common roadblocks to brotherly kindness: the penchants for judging people and for

---

impressing people. Concerning the latter, it says:

A third major enemy of love is vainglory—trying to impress others, using people to bolster our egos. This distortion is deeply rooted in our natures. So much so that Jesus warned against it in relationship to the areas of life in which man ought to be most sincere—his religious observances. "Be careful not to do your 'acts of righteousness' before men, to be seen by them. If you do, you will have no reward from your Father in heaven" (Matt. 6:1).

Jesus then applied this principle to giving to the needy (vv. 2-4), praying (vv. 5-15), and fasting (vv. 16-18).

The Pharisees of Jesus' day were so infected with this vainglory that it marred every facet of their lives. Jesus said, "Everything they do is done for men to see. They make their phylacteries wide and the tassels of their prayer shawls long; they love the place of honor at banquets and the most important seats in the synagogues; they love to be greeted in the marketplaces and to have men call them 'Rabbi'" (Matt. 23:5-7).

Our lives, like those of the Pharisees, are shot through with attempts to impress others. Advertising unabashedly appeals to that motive, urging us to think how impressed our neighbors will be when they see a brand new Chromemobile in our driveway. Or how heads will turn when we wear our new Johnny Tonight suit before admiring onlookers for the first time.

Many conversations between acquaintances are little more than an exercise in who can impress whom the most. . . .

This phenomenon even affects ministers' gatherings. Pastors ask one another about the success of their respective churches and grope in their minds for achievements for which they can be "humbly grateful."

Why do we behave this way?

Why are we so eager to impress?

Is it not that we want to feel within ourselves that we are important, and to have others recognize it too?

In itself the desire to be important is not wrong. But we can seldom establish our importance by announcing it to people. If we do manage to impress them, they are likely to resent us for making them feel small and unimportant. After all, they have a basic psychological need to feel worthwhile and of value just as we do.

The book points out that as we serve other people, we meet our own inner need to feel of value in a right way, a way that blesses our brother instead of uses him. We have now distinguished three aspects of brotherly kindness:

1. We must relate to people.
2. Our attitude must be one of love, acceptance, and forgiveness.
3. We must do others good in practical ways.

Practicing Brotherly Kindness

In the town of Joppa in the first century lived a woman named Dorcas. She was a person of humble circumstances, probably a widow with no close living relatives. Many people in her circumstances would have become lonely and bitter recluses. Others would have become pathetic social butterflies, desperately seeking some pleasures from life.

Dorcas, however, had added sisterly kindness to her faith, so she spent much of her time enjoying the fellowship of other widows.

But we've said that brotherly and sisterly love includes serving too. What could Dorcas do to serve others? Perhaps not much, but she could sew. There were poor people who needed garments—even children with no mothers to properly clothe their little bodies. So Dorcas began making clothing for the poor.

Then Dorcas got sick and died. About that time, the Apostle Peter was visiting a nearby town, so the Christians at Joppa sent an urgent message for him to come. When Peter arrived, he must have thought the pastor of the church had died, judging by how upset the people were. "All the widows stood around him, crying and showing him the robes and other clothing that Dorcas had made while she was still with them" (Acts 9:39).

Yes, Dorcas was truly mourned. Her passing was a loss because her presence had been an asset. What about you? Are you an asset to your Joppa? Have you added a practical brotherly kindness to your faith?

We cannot know for sure, but it's just possible that years later, as Peter wrote his list of character traits and came to brotherly kindness, his mind flashed back to a humble woman, a nobody really, whose sisterly kindness made her just too valuable to lose. Through Peter's prayer that day, God restored Dorcas to life.

Would you or I be worth added years? Or would our world be as well off without us? An unknown poet puts that kind of question to us:

I knelt to pray when day was done,
  And prayed "Dear Lord, bless everyone;
Lift from each saddened heart the pain,
  And let the sick be well again."

And then I woke another day
  And carelessly went on my way.
The whole day long I did not try
  To wipe a tear from any eye.

I did not try to share the load
  Of any brother on my road.
I did not even go to see
  The sick man just next door to me.

Yet once again when day was done,
  I prayed, "Dear Lord, bless everyone."
But as I prayed, into my ear
  There came a voice that whispered clear,

"Pause, hypocrite, before you pray,
  Whom have you tried to bless today?
God's sweetest blessings always go
  By hands that serve Him here below."

And then I hid my face and cried,
  "Forgive me, God, for I have lied.
Let me but live another day,
  And I will live the way I pray."

Yes, brotherly kindness does others good in practical ways. And yet there is so much more.

Brotherly kindness is the open door of hospitality so highly rated in Scripture and so often diminished in our culture.

Brotherly kindness is being true and loyal to a friend even

when that loyalty costs something, as it cost Jonathan when he sacrificed his hopes for the throne rather than be false to David.

Brotherly kindness is the concern for another's ministry that Barnabas showed when he brought Paul from obscurity in Tarsus to a place of ministry in the thriving church at Antioch.

Brotherly kindness is the kind of concern for a weaker brother shown by the same Barnabas when he insisted that John Mark should get another chance, despite his having failed on his first missonary journey.

Brotherly kindness is the love shown a weary Paul by the Christians at Rome who traveled all the way to the Three Taverns to greet him on his way to Rome not as a celebrity but as a prisoner (Acts 28:15).

Brotherly kindness is the gentle, meek restoring of a brother or sister who has fallen, when other people are condemning or gossiping and even tenderhearted Christians are staying away because the situation is just too sensitive and they don't know what to do.

Brotherly kindness is the touch that heals when someone's heart is breaking and it seems no one understands or even cares.

Brotherly kindness is noticing the young, the old, the poor, the unattractive. It is treating them as if they really are somebodies, even if no one else seems to think so and even if they don't think so themselves. It is knowing that in God's eyes they count, and so they count to you also.

Brotherly kindness is reaching out to someone who is hurting. It is sitting silently with someone who is suffering. It is praying for someone weighed down with discouragement, and then quietly doing something to cheer him.

Brotherly kindness is feeling Christ's own compassion and doing something about it.

"Add to your faith . . . brotherly kindness."

12
Should You Tell Them What You Really Think?

In our studies so far we've looked at three different dimensions of our lives.

1. We've looked inward. We've heard God say through Peter that we need to add goodness, knowledge, self-control, and perseverance to our faith.

2. We've looked upward, concerned that we not fall into the "horizontal heresy" of a self-improvement that stands alone. We've heard the Lord admonish us through Peter to add godliness to our faith.

3. We've looked outward. God has used Peter to impress on us that we must add brotherly kindness to our faith. We must involve ourselves with others, nurturing a spirit of love, acceptance, and forgiveness as well as helping people in practical ways.

4. What other direction is there to look, regarding character-building? None it would seem. Yet, there is one more trait in Peter's list. "Make every effort to add to your faith . . . love" (2 Peter 1:5-7). But love does not represent a fourth dimension of character, or a fourth direction in which to develop. No, love is the universal dimension; it is the necessay element to being right in *any* direction.

This love, which Peter lists as the seventh and last trait to add to faith, is not *phileo*, the tender affection of brotherly love. It is *agape*, the love that moved God to give His only Son, that whoever believes in Him has everlasting life (John 3:16). This is the love described in Paul's famous love chapter, 1 Corinthians 13.

Agape can be summed up, it seems to me, as *a commitment to care*. It is a dynamic, impelling, motivating force.

The first and greatest commandment is to love God with all our hearts, souls, and minds (Matt. 22:36-38). What is this but to care about Him most of all, and with all that we are? The second comandment is to love our neighbors as ourselves—to honestly care about the welfare of others as we do about our own (v. 39).

Caring about Others

Because brotherly kindness, or brotherly love, was the trait considered just before this one, let's ask first how the universal principle, love, relates to brotherly love, how *agape* relates to *philadelphia*.

The most common translation of *philadelphia* (in 2 Peter 1:7) is "brotherly kindness," probably because that simply reads better. To say, "Add to your faith . . . brotherly love; and to brotherly love, love" would sound awkward, redundant, confusing.

In the Greek, the words don't look alike, sound alike, or mean alike. *Agape* is wholly consistent with *philadelphia* as we have described it—an affectionate involving of our lives with others. However, *agape* goes beyond that. It includes caring about someone else's welfare, sometimes even at the cost of his warmhearted friendship.

Jim was one among a number of young people in our church who attended a distant Bible Institute. At the end of each school year when these young people returned to us, I asked them to present a Sunday evening service.

The senior member of the group at that time was named Webber, and I placed him in full charge. He worked out the service with the others, and I didn't even check it out. I didn't need to, for I had full confidence in him.

I was as surprised as anyone, on the evening of the service, when Jim arose to sing a solo. I'd been around Jim enough to know that he was tone-deaf and of course couldn't carry a tune.

The rendition by Jim that night was bad. I mean, it was a disaster. Any similarity between what Jim was "singing" and what the piano was playing was purely coincidental. The younger children were snickering, and many adults were shifting uneasily. Webber was looking at the floor lest he make eye contact with anyone in the audience, and poor Mrs. Porter, who loved good music, got up and walked out, obviously shaken.

After the service the kind people of the congregation told everyone including Jim how they appreciated the service and each one's contribution.

Since it was all over and done, I saw no need to take any action. Surely poor Jim had been humiliated enough so that he would never again sing in public. Even though the people had been too "kind" in their comments, surely his sister or his mother or *someone* would tell him.

The months went by and another school year came to an end. Again I asked Webber to plan a service. There was no need for me to check things out; I had full confidence in Webber. Then I remembered the previous year's painful experience and had second thoughts.

When I did look over the planned program, I was dumbfounded. Jim was to sing a solo. "What's this?" I asked. "Jim is going to sing again? I don't understand. I mean, I do believe in miracles, so it's possible I guess that a miracle has happened since last year. Is that the case? Is he now able to sing?"

Webber shook his head. "No, he still can't sing, but he thinks he can, and I don't have the heart to tell him he can't."

There was only one thing to do. Jim had to be told. I was his pastor, and I would have to tell him. After all, I was responsible for what went forth from the pulpit of the church. More important, it was not fair to Jim to let him continue in a state of delusion about his singing.

I arranged to meet with Jim. Webber had said Jim's heart was set on singing so I knew I would have to be gentle, and I tried to prepare him. "The Bible says, 'Faithful are the wounds of a friend,'" I began. "What I have to tell you may wound you, but it's for your good. You just can't sing Sunday night."

I explained to Jim the best I could that he did well at other things—even at leading singing, but that he just couldn't sing publicly.

Jim was silent and I had difficulty knowing how he was taking my admonition. When he did speak, I could hardly believe my ears. "All right," he said. "If you don't want me to sing, I won't sing. But I'm not going to give up my ministry in music just because of your opinion."

"It's not that I don't *want* you to sing," I said. "You *can't* sing. That's not my opinion. Just ask anybody. Ask Webber."

"I don't have to ask," Jim replied. "People have told me how they appreciated my ministry in song."

It was apparent from his tone and manner that Jim was offended. "You know, Jim," I said, "we ask you young people to present the service partly so that we can see how you've grown and profited from your Bible training. In your case, the test of what Bible school has done for you will show up much more in how you respond to being told the truth than in whether you can sing before a group."

Jim grunted an assent, but it was apparent he had turned me off. I had become his enemy because I had told him the truth.

I'm glad to say to Jim's credit that he later changed his attitude and decided I was his friend after all. But my point remains. Love is caring, and sometimes love means caring enough to risk rejection out of faithfulness to the welfare of another.

The Cost of Caring

Such love is not always reciprocated. We like to think that it is. We prefer to believe that if we love others faithfully, we will soon win their hearts. Often we will. But not always. After all, God loves every sinner with a perfect love. Yet that love may be scorned for years, even for a lifetime.

Paul knew what it was to love—to care even when he was misunderstood and his motives suspected. He loved the Christians of Galatia that way. They were easy to love, at first. They were so responsive to his preaching of the Gospel, so warm-blooded, enthusiastic, and outgoing that it was difficult not to love them.

When Paul first preached to these people, a bodily affliction had him in a low state physically and emotionally. Probably Paul's eyes were affected by his illness. They were most likely red and running with pus, for he was repulsive in appearance. With such a handicap, it was questionable whether his preaching would be effective.

But the Galatians received Paul with incredible warmth—"as if I were an angel of God, as if I were Christ Jesus Himself" (Gal. 4:14). Paul had been deeply moved, and still was even now some five years later as he was writing to them. It seemed they would have plucked out their eyes and given them to him, so great was their acceptance and love.

But those had been better days. Now they had cooled toward Paul. Others had come—Judaizers, who both maligned Paul and distorted the Gospel—and the Galatians were receiving these false teachers as warmly as they had once received him.

Paul tried to warn them, but by now his credibility had been severely undermined by his foes. Besides, his message was now unpalatable. To accept what the absent Paul was saying, the Galatians would have to reject what the persuasive teachers then present were saying. The warmth, enthusiasm, and openness Paul had liked so much in these people now worked directly against him. What could Paul do?

Love had only one answer. Paul had to tell them the truth even though, under the circumstances, it would take virtually a miracle of God for them to accept it.

So he wrote the Galatian letter. In it, he humbled himself and defended his standing as an apostle. He pleaded with them, appealed to them, and reminded them of the old times. He wanted so much to win them.

Yet he could not attempt to win them at the expense of the truth, for that would really be at their expense. If only they could see that. "Have I now become your enemy by telling you the truth?" he asked (Gal. 4:16).

Alas, it seemed that with these people, as with the Corinthians, Paul's experience was, "The more I love you, the less you love me" (2 Cor. 12:15, LB).

We don't know the sequel to the story—how much or how little favorable response Paul got. But we do see from his experience that love is caring, and true caring sometimes means we must risk being rejected.

When Does Love Confront?

We've said that *sometimes* true caring risks rejection by telling people the truth out of faithfulness to their welfare. This certainly does not mean we should go about setting everyone straight, making ourselves generally obnoxious, and then feeling like martyrs when people reject us.

Henry Jacobsen well depicted a young man who fell into this kind of error.*

It wasn't that he felt Superior to Other People. It was just that he Knew how Things should be done and was Willing to Share his Insight with others less Fortunate.

For instance, he knew how Harmful it is to Smoke Cigarettes, so he considered it his Duty to Warn his Boss against the Evils of Nicotine. By an odd Coincidence, he found himself passed up for a Promotion shortly afterward.

He realized that the New Dress his Girlfriend was wearing really didn't flatter her. He pointed this out to her in the Most Friendly Way—entirely, of course, for Her Benefit. After that the Girl had Previous Engagements whenever he tried to Get a Date.

He humbly admitted to himself that his Vocabulary was Excellent and he Made it a Point to pronounce Every Word according to Webster. When his Friends mispronounced a world like "camaraderie," he was always Glad to Set them

---

*From *Power for Living* © 1971 Scripture Press Publications Inc.

Straight—so that they wouldn't be embarrased by Mispronouncing the Word again. It was Unusual how Few Remarks his friends Made when he was around!

Before he bought a New Car, he made a Systematic Study of all the Models available. When he chatted with People who had bought Other Makes, he told them—for their own Welfare— just why His Car was better than Theirs, and how they had Made Mistakes in Judgment in their Purchases. He felt hurt that Some of them received this news Without Enthusiasm.

Out of the sheer Goodness of his Heart, he pointed out that People should not Park astride the Lines in the Parking Lot, should keep to the Right on the Sidewalk, should not Sing in the Choir if they couldn't Carry a Tune, and should Salute Properly when the Flag came by in a Parade.

His Help was not usually appreciated by Strangers, and once he had to Pick Himself Up off the Ground because some Stupid Oaf lost his Temper about being given a Civil Suggestion.

Our Young Friend could not understand why his Sound and Reliable Advice was not only Unappreciated but seemed to Make him less and less Popular. He remembered nostalgically a Time when he had had Nearly Six Friends. Then There was one, then none.

Moral: Maybe they aren't Doing It Right, but neither are they waiting for You to Set Them Straight.

It seems clear that love sometimes confronts those in the wrong, but perhaps more often it does not do so. If the rule were to point out wrong wherever it occurs, we would spend our time doing little else. And though we'd say we were doing it out of love, and for the other person's good, the result would usually be alienation.

Our doing good then would turn out something like the old joke about the boy scout helping an elderly woman across the street as his good deed for the day. She seemed very upset with the boy, and a bystander asked what was happening.

"I was just helping her across the street," said the boy.

"But why was she upset with you?"

"Because she didn't want to go."

In the two examples of appropriate confrontation given early in this chapter, both involved people in authority dealing faithfully with those in their charge. One question to ask when trying to decide whether to confront someone, then, might be:

Are you in a relationship of authority that makes it your duty to admonish that person?

If so, a second question is: *Will the person's state of growth permit him to accept your message?* Jesus told His disciples that He had much to say to them that they could not receive yet (John 16:12). He concerned Himself with whether they were in any condition to receive it. He would not dump a load of truth on them just because it was truth and they needed it.

Love is concerned for the welfare of the other, and it does no good to tell a person something he is totally unable to accept. All that does is alienate the one being told and make the critic feel he's done his duty and is free from any further responsibility.

A third question: *Is the issue of sufficient consequence that it requires action?* Certainly there is more reason to confront a person about using LSD than about smoking cigarettes. There is more reason to confront one who is listening to the Moonies than one who watches some worthless TV show.

A fourth test is a more subtle one. It relates to your deepest motivation. *Is this something you secretly enjoy, or something you would much rather not do?* If you secretly enjoy it, chances are it's motivated more by your own ego than by love. And if that's the case, remember, though you speak with the tongues of men and of angels in eloquent appeal to the wrongdoer, you are only "a resounding gong or a clanging cymbal" (1 Cor. 13:1).

"Add to your faith . . . love." So far as this relates to your brother or sister it requires an honest concern for his or her welfare. A concern that will withstand the scrutiny of the Holy Spirit Himself.

This kind of love, not being a response to lovable behavior on the part of others, clearly must come from within us. However, that does not mean we originate it. No, "love comes from God," as John writes (1 John 4:7). It is shed abroad in our hearts by the Holy Spirit (Roman. 5:5).

Lord, give us this love.

13
How Love Can Keep You Straight When All Else Fails

We must draw our study to a close. Not because everything has been said but because we can never say it all, just as we can never complete the work of building Christian character. We are to "possess these qualities in increasing measure" (2 Peter 1:8). We never have them in perfect fullness.

As we conclude then, we will content ourselves with saying a bit more about the seventh and most comprehensive trait, love. In addition, we will observe, ever so briefly, the weighty results Peter says will follow if we heed his character-building admonitions.

Loving Ourselves
I have no wish to offend those who dislike the term "self-love" and think it is no proper emphasis for a Christian. I do hope, however, to gain the agreement of all who love the Lord that Christians should care about being all they ought to be.

If we define love as caring, and if caring about our own character development is our duty, then "self-love" is a Christian virtue.

Loving yourself in this way is not self-indulgence, self-centeredness, or conceit. It is caring very much what kind of person you become. It is understanding that God made the person born to your father and mother on the date you celebrate as your birthday. This person belongs to God, who has placed in your hands immense power to develop that person or to stunt him.

If you care about and love this person God made, you will make every effort to add goodness, knowledge, self-control, and perseverance to your character. You will work and pray toward becoming a godly and loving person.

You will not find *this* kind of self-love in a self-indulgent person. He knows his indulgences waste his time, weaken his body, and only substitute for something worthwhile. The trouble is, he doesn't love himself enough to do anything about it. He should say, "Hey, I deserve better, and I'm going to see that I have better." Instead, he settles for less. He settles for crumbs, because he doesn't love himself enough.

My heart breaks when I see people who do not love themselves and who are hurting, hurting, hurting because of it. For one thing, all their relationships suffer, because one simply cannot live happily with others if he does not respect and accept himself.*

For example, abused people ordinarily do not love themselves. If they did, they would see how totally wrong such mistreatment is and would take measures to end these insults to God, which is really what they are (see Gen. 9:6 and James 3:9 for underlying principle here).

But didn't Christ meekly submit to all kinds of abuse? And doesn't the Bible say that those who suffer unjustly should follow His example? (1 Peter 2:18-23)

Yes, but with certain definite limitations. You see, submitting to abuse was redemptive in Christ's case. If that's true in our situation, we should do the same. More often,

---

*For an in-depth treatment of self-esteem, including insights into what destroys it and how to build it, read the author's book, *A True View of You*, © 1982, Regal Books, Ventura, CA 93003.

however, abuse is only destructive to all concerned. Christ was spit on. Does that mean a mother should let her children spit on her? Will that make them better children and her a better mother? Certainly not.

Her husband then—should she let him spit on her? Some would say so, because of the different authority relationship. He is over her, while she is over the children.

But authority is not a license to abuse. And submission does not require acquiescence to injustices no matter how monstrous they may be. For example, do you think a girl being mistreated sexually by her father would be wrong to take action to stop such abuse? Surely you wouldn't recommend that she "submit." That would hardly be an act of redemptive love.

So then, to allow yourself to go on being abused in a relationship is contrary to love, for it is detrimental to everyone concerned.

What kind of action should be taken is another question—probably one best decided with good counsel—but the abuse should not continue unchecked. Of course, it would cost something to change things, but that's what love is. It's caring enough to commit yourself to doing what's needed for your own welfare and that of others and the glory of God, in spite of the cost.

What we must understand is that love is not in conflict with itself. That is, love for God and for others does not require actions from us that are contrary to our own best interests.

Be clear on this. Certainly, loving may and will cost us in terms of hard choices and personal sacrifices. Love cost Jesus His life. But the cross was not only our means of redemption; it was also Jesus's path to His own greater glory (Phil. 2:8-9). Thus it was "for the joy set before Him" that Christ endured the cross (Heb. 12:2).

This is a heavy thought, and I almost feel we should follow it with "Selah," meaning "better take time out and think about that one for a while." By all means, feel free to do so.

Ready to Go On?

Since love seeks the highest good of the one loved, it involves giving up the lesser to gain the greater, as my friend Dale Galloway likes to say. Love for someone else will sometimes mean giving up your preferences for the sake of his or her welfare (Rom. 14:15-21).

Love for God will sometimes mean sacrificing your pleasures for His glory (1 Cor. 10:31).

True love for yourself will often mean denying what you want in favor of what you need.

In no case does love reverse the order. Love never sacrifices the greater to gain the lesser. Check it out:

- To sacrifice another's welfare to your preference is *exploitation*.
- To sacrifice your own welfare to another's whim is *abuse*.
- To sacrifice God's welfare (His glory) to your desires is *sin*.
- To sacrifice your welfare to God's cause is *fanaticism*. (It is impossible in the realm of truth since God is love and He cares always and without exception about your best good.)

Love means, then, that you can get off your guilt trip about doing legitimate things for your own welfare and benefit. It's OK!

We live in a time when people are more permissive generally about the pleasure they allow themselves. To a degree, this may be all right, but it's not at all what I'm talking about. I'm saying that it's not only all right but it's positively good for you to make the most of your life.

That's what love does; it makes the most of your life, not at anyone else's expense but to the glory of God and to the benefit of other people. If your dreams fit that pattern, don't listen when the devil cries, "Ego trip! Shame! Shame! You are out for your own advantage."

Instead, "add to your faith . . . love," including a proper love for yourself.

One Last Word about Loving God

Some contemporary teaching on the abundant life makes it

sound as if all will be prosperity, happiness, and health for a believer who has faith. That's as false as the old idea, in vogue not many years ago, that it is virtually sinful to enjoy such blessings.

Both ideas reflect a certain cultural captivity. In our time evangelical Christianity has gone from being a despised minority religion to being respected and admired, almost even dominant. That change has produced a gradual but dramatic effect on the group mentality of evangelicals. The "outs" have become the "ins," and their talk has gravitated away from a persecution mode to a prosperity mode.

Certain truths, however, remain constant. One is that God blesses His people and delights in their well-being. Another truth is that God is willing to demonstrate that His people's love is a true love that cares, even when it costs.

These two related truths are clearly set forth in Scripture. For example, Job enjoyed rich blessing from God both before and after his time of great trial. Satan's accusation was that Job only served the Lord for the benefits it brought him. "But put forth Thy hand now and touch all that he has; he will surely curse Thee to Thy face," Satan told the Lord (Job 1:11).

In other words, Satan said that if loving God cost Job something, Job would soon turn against God. The interesting thing is that God went along with the idea of testing Job in this regard.

Why?

Does God have to prove anything to Satan? Why not let the liar say what he wants and ignore him? I'm not sure I know the full answer to that question, but it's apparent that God chooses to test the love of His people and to demonstrate its validity.

Abraham is another example. He loved God, but that didn't mean he experienced only abundance and peace. Out of the blue one day, God imposed on Abraham's love an awful cost. "Take now your son, your only son, whom you love, Isaac . . . and offer him" (Gen. 22:2).

Dominating the entire landscape of the Bible is a cross on a hill. All the slopes of Scripture lead up to it or away from it. And the cross proclaims the same message as does Job's trial or Abraham's testing. There, loving obedience to His Father cost Jesus His life.

At some point, we can expect that our love for God is going to be tested. Faithfulness to Him will prove costly. We may never understand the reasons for His testing. Maybe it's mostly for our sake, for until we've faced a cost we don't really know whether we love God or not.

Merrilee had been a Christian long enough to know that sexual immorality was wrong. Just as she had been taught all 19 years of her life. But she was still curious—and impatient. So she began the rationalizing process, to convince herself that it would be OK.

"If I had done it before I became a Christian, the Lord would have forgiven me. So I'm sure He still would.

"Look at King David; he was a man after God's own heart.

"Just a casual one-night affair won't hurt the other person. A lot of people are used to that sort of thing.

"If any problems arise, there are plenty of clinics where a person can remain anonymous and be treated.

"No one needs to know, so my example won't be a stumbling block."

On and on she reasoned, over a number of weeks. Finally Merrilee had convinced herself that she could "get away with it."

One evening she was driving and saw a nice-looking hitchhiker just ahead. She flung a last, defiant challenge to God: "So, why shouldn't I?"

To her surprise an answer came back immediately: "Because I asked you not to."

Merrilee stepped hard on the gas pedal and sped past the waiting hitchhiker. The only reason she could not rationalize away had proved to be the only reason she needed. It just didn't square with her love for God.

Love is caring.

"Add to your faith . . . love."

The Roots of a Fruitful Life

We've devoted 11 chapters to considering the traits of character Peter says we should make every effort to add to our faith. Before that, in chapter 1, we warned of what may happen at the Judgment Seat of Christ if we lack these traits. Now, briefly, what happens if we faithfully develop them?

Peter writes, "If you possess these qualities in increasing measure, they will keep you from being ineffective and unproductive in your knowledge of our Lord Jesus Christ" (2 Peter 1:8).

Suppose you love blueberries. A few blueberries in your muffins or pancakes make a gourmet delight out of what would otherwise be ordinary food. And blueberry pie or blueberry cheesecake is your favorite dessert. Yum!

Then an idea strikes. The Bloomquists, down the road, produce beautiful blueberries right in their own garden. You have a few square feet of available ground in your backyard. Why not grow your own fresh blueberries in abundance?

Down to the local nursery you go. Three or four mature plants will be enough to supply your family, the nurseryman says. Then he starts making trouble for you. "Blueberries like soil rich in nutrients," he says, and begins reaching for some of the products he recommends. You only half grasp what he's saying: "slight acid soil . . . some super-phosphate or a complete fertilizer . . . well-mulched . . ."

"This guy just wants to sell fertilizer," you say to yourself. Well, you aren't interested in beautiful soil. It's blueberries you want.

"I'll take five plants," you say, mumbling something about getting whatever else you need later.

Now more than a year has passed. All five of those hardy plants that the nurseryman sold you have survived—and that's about all. The few small, scattered berries clinging bravely to the spindly branches are not worth picking.

Moral: You can't have good berry production without good soil.

As a Christian, you no doubt want a fruitful, productive life.

God wants that for you, too. But you won't become fruitful simply by trying. Even if you try harder, with five bushes instead of three or four.

Rather than working exclusively on the fruit front, give a little thought to the soil—your character—from which your daily life grows. The Scripture specifies what elements to add: goodness, knowledge, self-control, perseverance, godliness, brotherly kindness, and love—and then says these qualities will prevent barrenness.

There's one more piece of good news for character-builders. Christian character will not only make you fruitful and effective, as tremendous as that is. It will also provide you with a "rich welcome into the eternal kingdom of our Lord and Saviour Jesus Christ" (2 Peter 1:11).

Now that's quite a remarkable promise. God says that adding these seven traits will both make one fruitful in this life and happy in the next. Seems to me anything that great is worth more than just passing notice.

What do you think?

Stanley C. Baldwin offers seminars teaching these principles throughout the United States and Canada. If you would like to know when he is in your area, or if you are interested in sponsoring a seminar, conference, or broadcasts, write for full information:

Truth For Our Times
P. O. Box 101
Oregon City, Oregon 97045